ALL BETS ARE OFF

All Bets are Off

Horse Racing in Swansea

ROBIN CAMPBELL

GOMER

First Impression—2004

ISBN 1 84323 198 0

Front Cover illustration from: *The Illustrated Sporting &
Dramatic News*, April 23rd, 1887. John Sturgess was an
accomplished illustrator of books (eg *Racing* by the Earl of
Suffolk and Arthur Coventry) and magazines (eg *The
Illustrated Sporting & Dramatic News*). As a sporting and
animal painter he exhibited widely in the London galleries. He
spent many years studying the action and behaviour of horses
and their anatomy and was consequently able to capture the
reality, dangers and excitement of the hunting and steeplechase
field.

Printed in Wales by
Gomer Press, Llandysul, Ceredigion

Contents

Acknowledgements

I would like to thank the following for their help in the preparation of this book:

Firstly, Wray Vamplew for his invaluable advice and for contributing a Foreword; John Hayman for sharing his knowledge of the Clyne Valley and for persistently asking 'When's that damn book coming out?'; Marilyn Jones, Richard Brighton and the staff of Swansea Reference Library and Gerald Gabb and the staff of Swansea Museum who stubbornly refused to charge me for the pencils; Mrs Myers-Crump and the staff of Newmarket Library ; Mrs Dede Scott Brown of York Racing Museum and Library who patiently (I assume) dealt with my numerous enquiries; Miss James of Manselton Estate Office who provided both factual and anecdotal history, as well as an insight into the character of Richard Mansel Mansel; Mike Simpson of Deloitte and Touche (Cardiff) for making sense of some of the financial and legalistic terms, and Helen Reeves for cajoling him, sensing on each occasion that promotion was becoming a dimmer prospect; Dai Numbers, an old Cardiff racing fan who stood up and was counted; Heini Gruffudd for refereeing the bad-tempered game of bando, and Sarah Prest of Eclipse Pedigrees.

For providing the prints of the racecourse, I would like to especially thank Jeff Adams: for other photographs and prints, the unflappable Ken Dickinson; the Swansea exile, Carl Smith; Ray Stock, Colin Bevan, Alan Mogridge, Sir Philip Mansel, Bart and Grand National expert, Reg Green; Vernon Place, Jeremy Phillips and West Gamorgan Archive Service.

A special thanks to Tim Fearnside of the Geography Department at Swansea University for the map showing the position of the racecourse. May I also mention the late Gwilym Richards, *Cymro i'r carn*, who readily shared his extensive local knowledge with me and brought Bevan's farm to life.

Who else? Well, of course, Gill, Nia and Siôn, my family, who were enthusiastically indifferent. My thanks also to Jacob, the pedlar Jew, whose slow-burning tarred rope sparked off the inspiration for it all.

Foreword

Horse racing was the first truly national sport in Britain. Yet racing in Wales has not featured extensively in the literature of the sport. In this study of a particular locality Robin Campbell offers us a few well-constructed bricks to help fill the gap.

He shows that race meetings in early nineteenth-century Swansea were part of a broader leisure package that included public dinners, dances and evenings at the theatre for the well-to-do with drinking tents, gaming booths and itinerant entertainers for the masses. Despite changes in the organisation of racing that reduced the length of meetings and quickened the pace of the day, there was some continuity of expectations that racing was more than just watching the horses and placing a bet. This was especially true of those meetings, as in the early 1870s at Rhydydefaid, that were for non-thoroughbred horses. However, Robin Campbell also shows that, even at the major gate-money meetings that emerged late in the century, there were drinking facilities, shows and other entertainments. Indeed he demonstrates a special addition at Manselton in the coming of coffee stalls manned by the temperance movement.

But what makes this a real piece of history is that the author offers context. Sport is not isolated from what is happening around it in society. Racing in Swansea is placed not just within the developments of British racing but it is also shown as being influenced by local and regional economic events.

Wray Vamplew
University of Stirling

CHAPTER 1

Sport For All –
The Rise Of Commercialism In Sport

IT was March 1887 and from the grandstand on the hill above Manselton, spectators were greeted with a panoramic view over Swansea and the surrounding countryside. This magnificent new structure was the central point of an enclosed racecourse, an enterprise that seemed to symbolise a new era, both in sport and in the economy of Swansea itself.

A View from The Grandstand (from *The Illustrated Sporting and Dramatic News,* August 13th, 1887)
Such landmarks as the Third Glamorgan Rifle Range, Morris Castle and the Bonymaen School Boys' Reformatory could be observed from the grandstand. *The Cambrian* boasted that on a fine day the old town would compare with any place in Britain – 'Look at the swelling sea, the bold headland, the purple woods, the distant mountains . . . Trace the labyrinth of populous streets, the onward floating or the home returning ships, the mellow cornfields or the gorgeous pasture lands.'
(Courtesy WJ)

With the coming of the Industrial Revolution, the small Welsh town on the northern shore of the Bristol Channel had expanded from a minor medieval borough into a major coal-exporting port. During the nineteenth century Swansea had become the acknowledged king of the world copper industry with annual copper-ore imports reaching a peak of 95,361 tons in 1889.[1] A number of new steelworks added to Swansea's prosperity, as did industries such as tinplate manufacture and engineering, and in the final forty years of the century the town's population surged from 33,972 to 94,537.[2]

View of Landore, Swansea
(Photograph held by West Glamorgan Archive Service)

Such a large community demanded leisure activities and horse racing was one such outlet. It was not a new sport for Swansea for there had already been a racecourse on the Crymlyn Burrows and another one in the Clyne Valley. What was different about the Manselton venture, however, was that the course was enclosed and charged spectators for admission as a return on investment. The size of the grandstand alone, providing accommodation for 2,500 people,[3] reflected the rise of commercialised spectator sport in the latter part of the nineteenth century.

Sporting events had always been popular in Britain, often attracting huge crowds, but it was the entrepreneurs of the late nineteenth century who first provided fixtures or events on a regular basis – indeed, the new 'sports industry' undoubtedly became one of the great success stories of the late Victorian era.[4]

In pre-industrial Britain sporting events had been parochial, tending to be the focal point for annual community holidays. Very few people ever made a living out of sport and a largely impoverished population could not really be expected to pay admission to events such as racing, football or 'bando', the first mass spectator sport in Glamorgan. Any sporting occasion that required capital outlay had to depend on patronage – from publicans who could expect to sell ale at the event or from paternalistic landowners who might see the provision of sports as part of their social obligations.

Gambling was an integral part of these recreational activities. Foot racing had long been associated with Glamorgan, initially promoted by the gentry who backed their own servants in the races, footmen being professional runners who had been taken on to carry messages.[5] Interestingly, the apparent lawless and haphazard aspects of bando were temporarily sacrificed in the interests of those laying wagers demanding agreement on rules. Much of the sport and leisure activity in these pre-industrial days reflected the rural environment – horse racing, cockfighting, badger baiting. Land was a plentiful commodity and inter-village cricket and football games

BANDO

From about 1700 to 1850 bando was played in many areas of Wales but during the nineteenth century it became linked more and more with Glamorgan. At first sight bando is similar to the Irish 'hurley' and it was played on a large expanse of level ground, the wide sandy beaches being popular locations. 'Bando' was the name given to the bent sticks used to hit the ball. Such sticks were hard enough to knock the ball, as well as their opponents, into eternity. Players felt they had not done their duty unless they were laid up in bed for a fortnight after the contest. Usually the teams, which were followed by thousands of enthusiastic supporters, would play in their own colours (ribbons) and would number as many as 30 in each team. The size of the ball, sticks, the field and the goals would all vary from one game to the next. When one parish challenged another the rules were decided upon just before play started and it was particularly popular in the Cynffig-Margam district. The 'Margam Bando Boys', who played on Margam Sands, were celebrated in song in both Welsh and English and legend has it that every child over a year old in the town carried the familiar bando stick.

The game was also popular in Swansea and Neath, with thousands of the lower classes congregating on a Sunday during the summer months on the Crymlyn Burrows. According to Rev. W. Samlet Williams this 'foolish game' was the main sport in the area for most of the nineteenth century and contests were particularly fierce between the parishes of Llansamlet and Llangyfelach. The battles always ended in a massive brawl and the animosity engendered between communities lasted many years. The intensity of feeling is shown in the following verses which were handed down from one generation to the next:

> The wild boys in Coed-yr-Allt,
> Crying buckets and pulling their hair;
> Live, they do, above the sea;
> The merry boys of Llansamlet hammered them.
>
> Shôn, son of Twmi, like a bird,
> Scored the goal that beat the lads.
>
> (translated from the Welsh)

The sport lasted well into the twentieth century. Up until the 1930s, especially during the years of depression, it was a common sight in the valleys to see one street challenging another to a game of bando, or a variation of it.

'Bando' by Tecwyn Vaughan Jones, article in *Llafar Gwlad*, June 30th, 1985.
'Hanes A Hynafiaethau Llansamlet', by Rev. W. Samlet Williams, Dolgellau, 1908, p. 296-297.

were often played over many acres of countryside. Yet, whatever the sport, betting of a serious and petty nature was commonplace and was an essential part of the event.

Horse racing originated from rival owners wishing to prove the superiority of their respective mounts, cockfighting got rid of surplus male stock and badger baiting was an 'entertaining' method of pest control.

In Swansea, the Corporation had kept a bullring from 1723 until 1769. For many years bull-baiting was the most public and popular of all animal sports in Britain, linked with annual local holidays and characterised by much revelry. The sport was made illegal by an Act of Parliament in 1835 but its popularity had already declined in many areas by the 1790s.

The Beauties of Bull-baiting – painting by Henry Alken, 1821 in *A History of the English Turf* by Theodore Andrea Cook   *(Courtesy Newmarket Library)*

Before the Industrial Revolution working hours were determined primarily by the agrarian calendar. There was no such thing as a regular working-day, let alone a regular working-week, and many labourers would switch from one occupation to another as the demands for their services changed.

Nevertheless, the annual holiday was something that was eagerly anticipated by the whole community in these pre-industrial days. People lapped up the festive atmosphere at events like race meetings where drinking, dancing and sexual licence were the norm – arguably, the real professionals at this time were not the runners and riders but the publicans and whores who frequented the booths and taverns at racetracks such as Swansea.

The coming of industrialisation meant that work patterns had to change. The discipline of long and more regular hours took some time to establish itself in the minds of Welsh workers but by the middle years of the nineteenth century they had become well used to drudgery and exhaustion, largely unrelieved except by the plentiful supply of cheap alcohol.

As the century progressed, the consumption of tobacco, tea and sugar spread down the social scale. Industrialisation also brought with it a vast increase in readily available products such as cotton goods, cast-iron utensils and items such as soap. Workers gradually became used to the idea that 'time was money' and

The problem of beer drinking was a constant source of friction between masters and men. In Swansea the problem appears to have persisted for most of the nineteenth century :

When I bought these works, six years ago, I found the major part of the workmen very much addicted to excess in drinking, and scarcely a week passed in which we had not a serious breakage in the works, caused undoubtedly by the brains of the men being muddled with drink.

(an employer in Swansea, 1875.)

that their hard earned pennies could, indeed, buy them a certain amount of luxury goods. With it came the realisation that leisure time – once so abundant in pre-industrial Britain – might not be as plentiful, but that pleasurable diversions could be bought, paid for and enjoyed by all elements of society, not just the idle rich. It was something that the entrepreneurs also began to realise.

Advertisements for consumer goods – umbrellas, electro-plated novelties, jewellers, clothiers, house furnishers, wholesale grocers and cycles appeared weekly in local newspapers such as *Swansea, Mumbles and Gower*, 1904.
(Courtesy Swansea Reference Library)

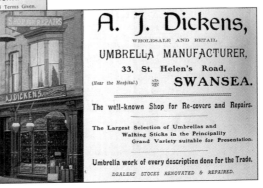

In Wales the influence of rigid nonconformity, together with significant social phenomena such as the temperance movement, soon polarised people into two irreconcilable lifestyles – the chapel and the public house. Edward Jones, 'Bardd Y Brenin', once lamented

> The consequence is, Wales, which was formerly one of the merriest and happiest countries in the world, is now become one of the dullest.[6]

The Hope and Anchor, Fisher St., Swansea, 1859

In 1880 there was one public house for every 27 other houses in Swansea and statistics show that between 1871 and 1873 a proportion of one person in 74 was convicted for drunkenness. W. R. Lambert describes the public house as 'the people's palace – the only free, non-esoteric, non-exclusive weather proof meeting place for the ordinary worker.'

(Courtesy City and County of Swansea: Swansea Museum)

The Reform Act of 1832 increased the political strength of the middle-class reformers and enabled them to influence legislation opposing events such as badger baiting and cockfighting that had been the staple leisure-time activity of the working man for many years. The Capital Punishment Amendment Act of 1868 also ended another popular 'blood sport', that of public executions. When 15,000 souls packed around the scaffold to watch Calcraft send Robert Coe, the Mountain Ash murderer, to his death in 1866, they had little idea that they were witnessing Swansea's last public hanging.

And yet, despite what seemed to be an eradication of many working-class pursuits, from the 1870s onwards most working people actually began to enjoy more free time. The right to be given a half-day on Saturdays was soon followed by the Bank Holiday Acts of 1871 and 1875, legislation that secured holiday status for Boxing Day, Easter Monday, Whit Monday and August Bank Holiday. There had been a significant shift in attitude from the propertied and moneyed classes.

Trips to the seaside to places like the Mumbles (visited by over 10,000 people on Whit-Monday 1882), brass bands,

The RSPCA, founded in 1824, became the chief agency for enforcing anti-cruelty laws and its private police force was bringing over 7000 prosecutions a year by the 1890s. Its leaders sought to reform the lower orders, rather than simply protect animals, and allied themselves to a host of middle-class movements seeking to persuade the working classes to behave in a 'proper' manner, based on religious conviction.

A branch of the RSPCA was established in Swansea in 1873. Ironically, its president, in 1886, was J.T.D. Llewellyn, Squire of Penllergaer, whose pack of hounds chased foxes and hunted otters. He also hosted a coursing meeting at Carn Goch, his annual sporting treat to the tenant farmers and gentlemen of the district. When organised by 'gentlemen' such activity was described as 'sport' by The Cambrian, but when the ordinary working man participated, it was 'uncivilised and barbaric.'

The poor at play in the 1820s and 1830s were widely regarded as idle, feckless, dissolute ruffians engaged in mindless, brutal and semi-criminal activities that were individually damaging and corrupting, a threat to order and a danger to society. The masses at play in the 1890s were generally accepted as reasonably well-behaved, exuberant maybe, but essentially harmless, engaged in legitimate and necessary relaxation and recreation in ways that might not be to the taste of the more genteel and educated classes but were tolerable as long as excesses were avoided and a proper separation of the classes was preserved.

FML Thompson[7]

Temperance reformers' attempts to change the notion of what constituted desirable physique coincided with the development of athletic sports in which the emphasis was on human, rather than animal participation. Athletic sports became an annual Whitsuntide event from the 1870s onwards at St Helen's cricket ground. In 1882 events included steeplechases, flat races, a tug-of-war and a three-legged race and were attended by a crowd of 4000.

football matches and Punch and Judy shows were all part of the entertainment. The late Victorian period saw a rapid rise in popular theatre, in particular the Music Hall, which soon became a significant feature in the life of working-class people.

So, too, did horse racing. Although in the early days horses made their own way to race meetings, led by their stable lads, the sport in Britain was revolutionised by the rapid spread

Advertisement for Madame Dolby's Music Hall Concert :
The Cambrian
September 28th, 1866
(Courtesy Swansea Reference Library)

20

of the railway network, the railway boom. From less than 1000 miles in 1839, the rail system had reached an incredible 13,500 miles by 1870. Racehorses were first transported by rail in 1840, which led to national meetings rather than mere local events, with spectators travelling all over Britain to attend certain meetings.

A host of new race meetings sprang up in the 1850s and 1860s, but they followed the traditional practice of extracting money from spectators via the stands, booths or other facilities rather than by charging for entrance. It was not until the rapid rise in workmen's wages in the 1870s and '80s that the time was ripe for sports promoters to set their sights beyond the beer tents and the gaming booths. Capitalists and entrepreneurs saw that money could be made out of people at play, just as it could be made out of people at work.

> *In broad terms there were two high-wage areas in Britain in 1850, London and the counties of northern England and part of the Midlands. By 1914 they had been joined by much of central and southern Scotland and by South Wales, where wages had risen faster than in Britain as a whole and where an increasing proportion of the region came to enjoy better than average earnings.*
>
> (E H Hunt, 1973)

All over Britain, in a variety of sports like cricket and football, grounds were now enclosed and entrance fees were levied. The sports industry had arrived. Market capitalism had come to the fore and the sports entrepreneurs, ably assisted by the sporting press, joined the music hall owners to provide a new leisure industry that could operate alongside the traditional activities of drinking and gambling. 'Following the horses', both literally and figuratively, became a major sporting activity for all.

One reason for the working class acceptance of commercialized sport was that it was prepared to accommodate, or at least tolerate, the traditional trio of alcohol, sex and gambling. Immorality and intemperance were 'part and parcel of the working class holiday', and drinking was an accepted feature of spectator sports.

Pay up and Play the Game: Professional Sport in Britain 1875-1914, Wray Vamplew, 1988

A long journey by road – an illustration by John Sturgess from *Racing*, by the Earl of Suffolk, 1886

(Courtesy the author)

CHAPTER 2

Races on the Crymlyn Burrows

T HE history of racing on the Crymlyn Burrows at Swansea can be divided into a number of distinct periods.

1790 to 1815

Horse racing in the Swansea area seems to have been well established by the 1790s. At that time it was organised by members of the elite Glamorgan society, almost as a hobby or private means of enjoyment. During the eighteenth century gentlemen in the county spent considerable time and money on activities such as stock breeding, horses and hounds, all of them seen as symbols of gentry status. As guests at Lord Vernon's Briton Ferry estate they would have found the nearby Crymlyn Burrows an ideal venue for contesting the merits of their respective mounts. Backing their horses with a wager was just one more element in the game.

The Races on the Burrows first appeared in the Racing Calendar in 1803 and, by racing under Jockey Club rules, Swansea was hoping to join several well-established racecourses in South Wales, venues such as Cowbridge, Monmouth, Cardiff and Haverfordwest. The greater Welsh families had, for many years, visited Newmarket and Epsom while they were in London for the season and the newly ascendant gentry families that emerged in Glamorgan after 1760 were keen to live up to the aristocratic traditions of recreation and leisure – albeit within their home county.

IN THE OLDEN DAYS –
Note that the fashion at that time was to dock the horses' tails.
The Analysis of the Turf, by J Fairfax-Blakeborough, Philip Allan 1927
(Courtesy Newmarket Library)

Once established, the annual Race Week on the Crymlyn Burrows quickly became an integral part of the entertainment on offer at Swansea as the town assumed a new role as a seaside resort during the late eighteenth and early nineteenth centuries. Sea bathing was suddenly in vogue as medical men discovered and expounded its restorative qualities. The leisured classes also craved amusement, however, and consequently 'the successful seaside towns quickly became centres of fashion, entertainment and gambling.'[1]

There was no better place for fashionable young ladies and gentlemen to display themselves than at the races. Ordinaries – in other words public meals – balls, public breakfasts and evenings at the theatre provided the gentry with further opportunities to confirm their position as leaders of society.

Much of the early organisation of Swansea Races seems to have been in the hands of James Simpson, Clerk of the Course between 1807 and 1815. In April each year he would place a front-page advertisement in *The Cambrian* newspaper, inviting subscribers to Swansea Races to a meeting at the Ferry House 'for the purpose of making the necessary arrangements for the ensuing races.'[2] The following week another advertisement would give the race programme and the rules of the meeting.

Races at this time were run over three days and from 1804 onwards were usually held in July. In 1814 and 1815 there

Advertisements from *The Cambrian*, August 6th, 1808, including THE FIRST RACE DINNER and the opening of the new season at the NEW THEATRE, SWANSEA

(Courtesy Swansea Reference Library)

Burrows Ferry House, later known as The Beaufort Arms, the meeting place for Swansea Races subscribers in the early 1800s : *A Pictorial History of Swansea*, W. C. Rogers, Gomer, 1981

(Courtesy City and County of Swansea: Swansea Museum)

A MEETING of the SUBSCRIBERS to the SWANSEA RACES will take place at the Ferry-House, Swansea, on Tuesday, the 19th instant, at two o'clock, for the purpose of making the necessary arrangements for the ensuing Races.

The attendance of every Subscriber is earnestly requested, as the number and description of the Plates will be settled on that day, and advertised in the next Racing Calendar.

C. R. JONES, Esq. } Stewards.
S. HOMFRAY, Esq. }

Dinner on Table at Four o'Clock.

Advertisement from *The Cambrian*, April 16th, 1808 – requesting the attendance of Subscribers to the SWANSEA RACES

(Courtesy Swansea Reference Library)

were only two days' racing, however, seeming to indicate that by this time there was a waning of interest from among County society.

The early races were almost completely dependent on patronage, although tradesmen were expected to pay a week in advance to erect their booths and blacksmiths had to contribute half a guinea to any race in which they were plating (or shoeing) a horse.[3] Most of the prizes consisted of plates of £50 or more, possibly a silver or gold cup, paid for out of the race fund by subscribers or presented by wealthy individuals. County MPs and Stewards – a mixture of landed gentry and industrialists – were expected (and were usually more than happy) to donate prizes.

Sir Charles Morgan, Bart., liberally furnished public breakfasts and Ordinaries, offering the finest venison and fruits from Tredegar House. Such occasions were used by the Stewards to exact promises of subscriptions and prizes for the following year's races – it meant courting the company in a somewhat sycophantic manner but was also, usually, highly successful.

Such was the patronage in these early days that balls and Ordinaries took place on each of the three days. In a good year about 200 notable ladies and gentlemen could be expected to dance the night away in the Town Hall and *The Cambrian* was always eager to furnish its readers with lists of the company that had arrived in Swansea – everyone from minor aristocracy, gentry and doctors to churchmen and many an eligible 'Miss', no doubt accompanied by protective mamma or married sister.

No figures are available for the number of working people who attended the races, a high point in their social calendar as well as the gentry's. However, Miss Elizabeth Isabella Spence talked about 'the concourse of hundreds of spectators . . . and booths scattered in all directions' when she visited the races in 1808.[4]

The races were clearly leisurely affairs. The Racing Calendar shows that the 1803 meeting was held in the first week of August with only one race being decided on each day. In order to draw out proceedings races were run in heats, a device used to obtain a full day's racing from a limited supply of horses. The winner of an event was the first to win two heats, something that often required four or more races. Even so, only eight contests took place over the three days, involving half a dozen gentlemen, each with one horse.

Matches were an integral part of the early races, the sum of 200 guineas being at stake when Mr King's three-year-old chestnut filly, Glamorganshire Lass, beat Captain Jones's four-year-old Maria over the last half mile of the course in 1810.[5]

AN OLD RACECOURSE
The Analysis of the Turf, by J Fairfax-Blakeborough, Philip Allan, 1927
(Courtesy Newmarket Library)

As more owners with more horses were attracted to the races the number of sweepstakes in the programme grew rapidly. Twenty entries at a cost of £50 each made a prize worth running for. As with the rest of Britain, Swansea followed the general pattern of horse racing with an increasing trend towards sweepstakes where anyone with a second-rate horse and the entry fee could try to win the prize money. In 1810 two sweepstakes alone attracted thirty subscribers, with the 5 guinea stakes, the last event of the three days, being the first example of a 'selling race' at the Burrows.[6] It was a far cry from the days when a small band of the County elite would challenge each other in an unhurried affair in an event over which they had total control.

Sweepstakes first appeared at Swansea in 1805 but plates and matches dominated proceedings until 1811, which saw more sweepstakes and free handicap stakes than any other type of race. An increasing number of races came to be contested over shorter distances. It was obvious that the nature of horse racing at Swansea had changed for good.

1823

The races of 1815 were the last to be held for eight years, despite efforts to organise the event in 1816 and 1818. There are several possible reasons for the failure. The landed gentry may have withdrawn their patronage because sweepstakes and handicap races now filled most of the race card. Not only was there the risk of breakdown to valuable horseflesh but, due to handicapping, there was now no guarantee that the best horse would actually win a race. Bigger fields also meant that it was easier to 'pull' a horse or spoil a favourite's chance by foul riding.

The original intention of sweepstakes may have been to encourage breeding of first-rate horses but its growing popularity was a sign that commercial profit was now the driving force with owners risking less for the chance of winning more.

Another factor in the failure of the races was that landed families (and the newer industrial gentry) were, after the close of the Napoleonic wars, not so dependent on British resorts to supply them with recreation. Many wealthy people now felt safe to return to Europe for their pleasures and did so in ever increasing numbers.

Swansea was undergoing a significant change during these years. By the 1820s the population of the town had increased to 10,000, mainly as a result of the new copper works in the area. The industry employed a thousand men and supported, perhaps, ten times that number in the coalmines and docks that were inextricably linked to the copper trade. Many people felt that it was trade and commerce that would bring wealth to the town, not the summer visitors who came to parade on the sands and bathe in the waters of the Bristol Channel.

There were those who sought to 'hedge their bets', however, and have the best of both worlds. When the Swansea Races were revived, however briefly, in 1823, the Corporation paid for a plate of 50 sovereigns while the tradesmen of the town subscribed the same amount for another plate.[7] Whereas the civic leaders were pandering to the well-heeled hypochondriac visitors whose idea of a perfect day was to dodge the seaweed on their way to the bathing machines,

Bathing Machines at Swansea.
(Courtesy City and County of Swansea: Swansea Museum)

there was no doubt that the publicans were casting their eyes towards the growing number of industrial workers who would certainly abstain from work (but not drink) for the few days of the race meeting.

Despite an advertisement that appeared in March 1823, asking for gentlemen who were interested in promoting alternate races at Cardiff and Swansea, there seemed to be little enthusiasm from the eastern part of Glamorgan.

It would appear that there was a certain amount of bad blood between Swansea and Cardiff Corporations over the issue. *The Hall Day Minute Book* of 20th September, 1822 tells us that

> The burgesses decide to give a Plate of Fifty Guineas for Horses bred in South Wales carrying the King's Plate weights in any years when the Race shall be held in Swansea . . . they will contribute a Sum towards the Cardiff Races equal in amount to any contribution made by Cardiff Corporation towards the Swansea Races . . .

1834 to 1847

In 1834 Sylvanus Padley, Portreeve of Swansea, chaired a meeting to decide on the best means of re-establishing the annual races. Within three weeks over £150 in subscriptions had been raised.[8]

It was the tradesmen of the town, not the landed families of eastern Glamorgan, who were behind the enterprise – brewers and publicans, saddlers, farriers, and tanners. Messrs Newcombe and Bedford, proprietors of the theatre, together with various jewellers, perfumers and drapers were happy to offer their services to those who would undoubtedly flock to the town for the event. Local gentry and industrialists saw it as their duty to promote the town and as long as they remained at the head of the social ladder, were happy to see the masses have their fun. The races were hereafter to be known as 'The Swansea and Neath Races', and as if to cement this new-

SWANSEA and NEATH RACES
WILL TAKE PLACE
On the 17th and 18th of AUGUST next.

FIRST DAY.

THE GLAMORGANSHIRE STAKES of Twenty
Sovereigns each, with £50 added.

	yrs. st. lbs.
Mr. Fredericks names *Barny Bodkin*	6 9 1
Mr. Miers names *Nell Gwynne*	6 8 13
Mr. J. H. Peel's *Changeling* .. .. .. aged	8 8
Mr. J. J. Bristow's *Dr. Slop*	3 7 5

Ch. g. by *Rossini, Timothy, Circe, Kendal,* and *Brother to St. Nicholas,* pay 5 Sovereigns each, having declared forfeit. Mr. Moggridge and Mr. Parr are Subscribers but did not name

A PLATE of FIFTY POUNDS, for any Horse, Mare, or Gelding. Three-year-olds, 7st. 7lbs.; four, 8st. 7lbs.; five, 9st.; six and aged, 9st. 5lbs.; Mares and Geldings allowed 3lbs. One Sovereign entrance or double at the post. Heats once round.

A SWEEPSTAKES of FIVE SOVEREIGNS each, for Horses not thorough-bred, with added. Three-year-olds, 9st.; four, 10st. 10lbs.; five, 11st. 5lbs.; six, 11st. 12lbs.; aged, 12st. Once round. The winner to be sold for £100, if demanded in the usual way. Maiden Horses allowed 5lbs.

A SCURRY STAKES of THREE SOVEREIGNS each, for Horses of all denominations, with £15 added. Three-year-olds, 8st. 5lbs.; four 9st. 10lbs.; five, 10st. 9lbs.; six and aged, 11st. 2lbs. The winner to be sold for £50, if demanded within half an hour after the race. Once round.

A SADDLE and BRIDLE for PONIES.

SECOND DAY.

A PLATE of FIFTY POUNDS, for any Horse, Mare, or Gelding. Three-year-olds, 7st. 3lbs.; four, 8st. 7lbs.; five, 9st.; six and aged, 9st. 5lbs. The winner of first day's Plate, or Glamorganshire Stakes, to carry 7lbs. extra; if of both, 14lbs. extra. A winner of £100 at any one time, or Gold Cup, to carry 7lbs. extra, in addition to the other extra weights, but no horse to carry more than 14lbs. extra. Mares and Geldings allowed 3lbs. One sovereign entrance or double at the post. Heats once round.

A SWEEPSTAKES of THREE SOVEREIGNS each, for Galloways and Ponies under 13 hands, one sovereign forfeit, with £10 added. Ponies to carry catch weights. The Galloways to be entered before nine o'clock on the evening of the 17th, and to be handicapped by the Stewards, or whom they may appoint. Three to start or no public money will be given. Heats once round.

A HANDICAP of FIVE SOVEREIGNS each, two sovereigns forfeit, with £25 added, for the beaten Horses at these Races. To be entered and handicapped by the Stewards or whom they may appoint, immediately after the Race for the Plate. Three to start or no public money will be given.

A TROTTING MATCH for TEN SOVEREIGNS, added to a Sweepstakes of One Sovereign each, subject to the usual conditions in Trotting. The Horses to be handicapped by the Stewards, or whom they may appoint. The Horses to be entered on the evening of the 17th.

A SADDLE and BRIDLE for Ponies. The winner on the first day not allowed to start.

L. W. DILLWYN, Esq. M.P. } Stewards.
W. WILLIAMS, Esq. }
J. G. RICHARDS, Clerk of the Course.

RULES TO BE OBSERVED.

No Horse to stand at any Stables but those of Subscribers, or not entitled although a winner.

No Smith allowed to charge, unless a Subscriber, or not entitled although a winner.

Persons wishing to erect Booths, must apply to the Clerk, who will appoint a day to let the ground, when the booth-money must be paid, or the ground to be let to another.

All Dogs found on the ground will be destroyed.

All Horses to pay 10s. 6d. for Scales and Weights, and all winners One Guinea.

Horses to be entered for the First Day's Plate and Stakes at the Mackworth-Arms, at the hour of eight o'clock, on the evening of the 15th. For the Second Day's Plate and Stakes, at th...

Announcement of the 1836 August
Race meeting, with a detailed
description of races and prizes.
(Courtesy City and County of Swansea :
Swansea Museum)

found municipal affection, the role of Stewards was filled by John Henry Vivian, local copper master, and Frederick Fredricks of Duffryn, Neath.[9]

John Henry Vivian, Copper Master and Member of
Parliament for Swansea and District 1832-1855
(Courtesy City and County of Swansea: Swansea Museum)

The races of the 1830s and 1840s reflected the vitality and energy brought by industry and recent municipal reform but lack of money was always a significant problem. The organisation was very business-like, accounts for the year 1840 showing a loss of £18.11s 1d, after bills had been paid for repairs to the racecourse, to the police for clearing the course, and the paying of various stakes.[10] Mr Thomas Shepherd was both Treasurer and Secretary and Clerk of the Course.

Training in the 1830s , an illustration from *Sport of Kings*, Ralph Nevill, Methuen, 1926
(Courtesy Newmarket Library)

The issue of unpaid subscriptions must have been an intolerable burden because in 1843 he fell off his horse and was replaced by Mr Morgan Price – who had the distinct advantage of a Committee of Management to help him in his task. Funds remained low, however, and requests were made to both gentry and tradesmen for support. Generous donations were received from people like Sir Josiah John Guest, Lord Adare of Dunraven Castle and CRM Talbot. The Ladies of Glamorgan provided a Silver Cup on five occasions between 1841 and 1847 but the man who really stood out as far as patronage was concerned, was the 'Colossus of Copper', John Henry Vivian. He regularly subscribed £25 to the races as well as giving the same amount in prize money to the Welter Stakes (races involving heavyweight riders). His greatest delight, however, seems to have been in providing public breakfasts at the Mackworth Arms.

The Mackworth Arms (Mackworth Hotel) in Swansea
(Courtesy City and County of Swansea: Swansea Museum)

In 1838 a grandstand and booth was erected on the course by Evan Evans of the Grant's Arms in Neath. The entrance fee was 1/6d for the front seats and 1s for the back. Evans made himself a small fortune by keeping the well-heeled, well-oiled in the comfort of his booth next door! Grandstands provided a type of social exclusivity at the races – giving the 'nobs' a clear view of any fisticuffs amongst the peasantry, while at the same time, protecting them from the said rabble.

Charging a fee of one guinea for the proprietors of gambling booths, beer tents and food stalls to erect their tents or premises provided good income for the race committee. Stable keepers who took in horses and the smiths who plated them were also expected to contribute. For each horse entered there was a fee of half a guinea in order to pay for scales and weights while the winner of each race was expected to donate an extra guinea as an additional contribution! From 1836 selling races became part of the programme, with a hoped-for spin-off for the race fund whilst the lucky winner of the 1838 Glamorgan Stakes was expected to pay £5 towards the repair of the racecourse. Between 1845 and 1847 the conditions of ten different races required the victor to contribute to the race fund, something that was widespread practice on the British Turf at the time.

No attempt was made to charge for admission to the race meetings that had quickly established itself as a traditional local holiday. If spectators wanted to buy food or drink at the course then that was up to them, but it was a basic ingredient to the day that it should be a free event. Most people in the town excused themselves from work for a few days and the annual, if basically unofficial, holiday was eagerly anticipated by everyone.

SELLING RACES

Roger Longrigg informs us that the first selling race on record took place in 1689. In the early years at the Crymlyn Burrows, it appears that there was no profit in it for the race fund. In the 5 guineas sweepstakes of 1810, the conditions stated that the winning horse was to be sold for 60 guineas and that the owner of the second horse had the first entitlement to buy. Selling races later became a vital source of revenue for race committees. At Swansea in 1855, for example, Master Frederick, the winner of the Hurdle Race, was bought for £205, one of the conditions being that any surplus over £60 should be given to the racecourse.

The crowd at the 1835 races was estimated at 8,000 – a remarkable figure in view of the fact that the railway system had not yet reached Swansea and the population of the town was only 13,265.[12] However, for most of the people who thronged to the course the races were incidental. Alcohol, gambling and sex were what they had come for – and a tidy bit of violence on the side. A pitched battle between the 'boyos' of Neath and the military stationed in Swansea became, for a while, almost an annual event. As one local described it:

'We saw flashes of metal flying about in the sunshine, bludgeons descending on the heads of combatants, and a general melee . . . blood was everywhere, and the combatants, more particularly the Neath men, presented a ghastly spectacle. The disturbance, which practically became an absolute riot, lasted a long time.'[13]

Of that crowd of 8,000, the gentry and the 'fashionables' would have numbered a few hundred at the most. The distinction between the social classes would have been heightened by the language they

... scenes of vice and profligacy ...

Not everyone joined in the carefree mood of the races. Popular pastimes, favoured by the upper and lower classes alike, had been vigorously attacked by the temperance movement since the end of the eighteenth century. Middle class social reformers tried to impose their standards of conduct on society but failed to a large degree. Joseph Tregelles Price, Quaker, and Master of the Neath Abbey Ironworks felt compelled to insert a mini-sermon in *The Cambrian* newspaper directly underneath an advertisement for the 1836 Swansea and Neath Races.

In contemplating the approach Races this year, I have been induced to take a retrospect . . . of what in past years has been their obvious consequence – neglect of duty on the part of the workmen to their employers, to their families and to themselves. I hear of booths being erected, where beers and spirits are supplied, and of the encouragement afforded on these occasions to excess in drinking, gambling, and other scenes of vice and profligacy.

FLOTSAM AND JETSAM – an early 19th century racecourse. Note the variety of peripheral activities in the foreground, including band members – a fiddler and a trumpeter – a broadsheet seller, a beggar, a food vendor and a pair of pugilists in an improvised boxing ring. *The Analysis of the Turf*, by J Fairfax-Blakeborough, Philip Allan, 1927

(Courtesy Newmarket Library)

spoke. The vast majority of the copper workers and Llansamlet colliers, for example, would have been monoglot Welsh-speakers, as probably would have been the Neath men at that time.

Matches – races between individual horses and owners – had been a vital ingredient of horse racing in the days when the sport had been an aristocratic pastime. By the 1830s and 1840s, however, such matches had largely disappeared. The bulk of the races were now sweepstakes, either weight-for-age or handicap. The distance for the races now tended to be two miles, just once around the course, rather than the four-mile endurance test. The prizes on offer were not great but for owners and spectators alike there was always the prospect of a 'flutter' on the horse of your choice.

If the working classes didn't earn enough to speculate very often, the tradesmen of Swansea certainly did. They quickly became the backbone of the races, establishing a Derby Club in 1843, which met in the Rose and Crown Inn, Wind Street, and the Shades Tavern in Salubrious Place. At their annual dinners, sweeps for the

WEIGHT FOR AGE

Weight-for-age races are based on the principle which allows for the differences in the abilities of horses caused by maturative factors. The younger horses carry less weight than the older and more mature animals. In the nineteenth century there appear to have been three varieties of weight-for-age races

1) Weight-for-age proper, in which animals of the same age carried the same weight, such as the Coventry Stakes at Ascot for two-year-olds and the five "classic" races for three-year-olds.
2) Races such as the Middle Park Plate at Newmarket, where horses of the same age carried the same weight but where there were penalties for previous successes.
3) Races in which horses of different ages met and were weighted according to a table drawn up by Admiral Rous, who emerged as 'Dictator of the Turf' in the early 1860s.

principal English race meetings would be drawn and prizes presented. The Crymlyn Burrows meeting was the highlight of their year, their very own Derby or St Leger, when they could gamble to their hearts' content. Horse racing and gambling clearly went together.

By using a system of heats, seventeen contests were squeezed out of a two-day race card comprising nine races in 1843, bettered only in 1847 when there was an opportunity

A RACECOURSE OF THE PAST, *Sport of Kings*, Ralph Nevill, Methuen, 1926
(Courtesy Newmarket Library)

to speculate on eighteen races. It was certainly a far cry from 1805 when nine races over three days reflected the lifestyle of a gentry class who seemed proud to be idle.

The 1847 meeting was deemed to be the best that had taken place for many years. Money was still a problem, however, and despite the success of Race Week it was felt that some of the gentlemen of the county were not pulling their weight. Many subscriptions were not forthcoming and the races simply ground to a halt. It was to be eight years before they were run again.

1855 to 1858

The Secretary of the 1855 Swansea Races was the dynamic, if controversial, Thomas Bullin. Among the ordinary folk he would be remembered for years as a despicable toll-farmer, coming to South Wales about 1830 and holding gates in all parts of the area. He was certainly energetic, and if the races could no longer rely on aristocratic or even gentry patronage then Bullin was the man for the job. He could exact subscriptions from unenthusiastic members of the wealthy classes in the same uncompromising way that he had held to ransom the poor Welsh farmers at the Turnpike gate.

The 1855 and 1856 races were successful enough, although the *Swansea Journal* observed that in 1856 'the number of equestrians were fewer this year than we can remember on any former occasion.'[15] The important dignitaries that papers like *The Cambrian* wanted and needed in order to give the races a certain 'éclat' did not really appear, and Ordinaries at the Mackworth and the Packet Hotel attracted only 30 or 40 gentlemen. Local people still flocked to their meeting in their thousands and in 1856 a new grandstand was erected on the course. By this time the Committee was charging for

'The Rebecca Rioters': the original cartoon appeared in *The Illustrated London News*

During the Ordinary, at the end of the first day's racing in 1855, the self-important Thomas Bullin, dressed for hunting, replies to a toast in his honour.

Mr Bullin (who was still attired in his 'scarlet,') felt greatly obliged to all of them for the compliment they had paid him. Any thing which he had done in connection with the races was to him a pleasure and not a trouble, and perhaps afforded him more real enjoyment than any gentleman present. He was always happy to serve them at any races, for his whole soul was in the turf. He did like it all with his heart and soul, and nothing gave him more pleasure than to be on a good horse. He went to the races determined to win – he won a small cup that day, and he hoped to win another tomorrow. He would continue the races just as many years as they chose to subscribe. He would do the working part of the business if they would subscribe the money. When he served under two such able stewards as their Mayor and their Member, he thought he was highly honoured. He took upon himself to solicit subscriptions. Some people said he would not succeed – but they did not know Tom Bullin: however he did succeed and the stakes were now ready whenever the winners chose to call for them. In conclusion, he would tell them he was willing to go as far forward with the races as they chose, but he would not go a step backward. (Cheers) He would only add – get such good stewards for next year and then they would get £500 at least. (Applause.)

The Cambrian, August 24th, 1855

admission to the ground, although only for those with saddle horses and carriages. The charge of 1s and 2/6d respectively was made not only to help boost the race fund but also to comply with the 1853 Betting Act.

It is doubtful whether the Committee ever seriously considered charging a general admission fee, though with a crowd of 6000 attending in 1855 the matter must, at least, have been raised. It would have been easy to collect money

from the gentry, congregated in the vicinity of the stand, but totally impractical along the miles of unenclosed wilderness that constituted the Burrows. And besides, nobody wanted to risk provoking a riot.

The coming of the railway in 1850 was significant for Swansea and Neath Races. In racing terms it meant that the spectator catchment area had widened considerably. Horses could now race outside their traditional local circuits, being speedily and economically transported on the new railway system. A considerable portion of the crowd in 1855 were described as 'strangers',[16] while the following year many of the jockeys were household names in the racing fraternity.

The death of John Henry Vivian in 1855 was a great setback to the races. He had been involved since about 1814, when he was Steward, and his patronage had served as a copper-bottomed guarantee. His son, H. Hussey Vivian, acted as Steward in 1856 but he was clearly unwilling to go the distance as his father had done. Perhaps Victorian respectability was starting to influence the local aristocracy.

The Committee had also had enough, each of them committing up to three months of their time every year to organise the races, and the 1858 event was the last of the Swansea and Neath Races to be held under Jockey Club rules. As a last act the grandstand was sold by auction on the second, and last, day of the meeting.

THE GRAND STAND-

Mr. THOMAS GLOVER
WILL SELL BY AUCTION,

On TUESDAY, the 31st day of AUGUST, 1858, the day of the Swansea Races, on CRYMLYN BURROWS, as now erected,

THE GRAND STAND, either with or without the Canvass. Size, 35 ft. ⋈ 22 ft. The Scantling and Planks are nearly new, and, if required, can be immediately used for building purposes.

This Sale will take place at 11 o'clock Forenoon precisely. And at the Back of the GREYHOUND INN; Caer-street, SWANSEA, on the same day, at 6 o'clock Afternoon precisely, another Lot of prime Scantling and Plank, for same uses.

The auction of The GRANDSTAND, on site, signalled the end of formal race meetings on the Crymlyn Burrows in the summer of 1858 : *The Cambrian*, August 27th, 1858
(Courtesy Swansea Reference Library)

A few 'spirited individuals' cobbled together a one-day event on the Crymlyn racecourse in 1861 but it proved to be a miserable affair. Two years later the Vale of Neath Railway had opened a line over the Burrows to Swansea Docks, thus spelling the end of the old racecourse and, with it, a way of life that, as the years went by, fewer and fewer people would ever remember or dream about.

CHAPTER 3

The Clyne Valley Races

EVEN before the demise of the Crymlyn Burrows racecourse there had been other racing events in the west of Swansea. In January 1857, Mr Abel Vivian, landlord of the Red Lion Inn at Blackpill, organised a modest day's racing on the nearby sands. Thomas Bullin acted as judge, his horse Forester carrying off the prize in the last race of the day.

Despite the obvious benefits of the location, no further races were held in this part of Swansea until Vivian revived them in 1860. The Oystermouth Railway had recently opened for passenger traffic and that meant, with trains running every half-hour on that day, easy access for spectators.[1] The following year races were held on Whit Tuesday and hundreds of racegoers were treated to an eventful day.

There were only two races on the card and the first, the Oystermouth Handicap, did not fill. Four horses started for the

RED LION INN,
HALF-WAY HOUSE TO THE MUMBLES.

A. VIVIAN begs to return his grateful thanks to his Friends and the Public for the Patronage bestowed upon him since he has entered upon the above INN; and begs to inform them that his large SALOON will be ready on the Green, opposite his House, Fronting the Bay of Swansea, for the reception of TEA PARTIES, &c., and will continue every Tuesday and Friday, during the Summer.

Tea and Ham at One Shilling each.

Newspaper advertisement from *The Cambrian* of June 1856, for the public use of Abel Vivian's SALOON at The Red Lion Inn
(Courtesy Swansea Reference Library)

The Red Lion Inn, Blackpill, as it would have appeared in the early nineteenth century.

Volunteer Handicap but then the jockey Walters, who won the first two heats on Swalcliffe, was disqualified for dismounting before coming to the scales. An unfortunate incident occurred during the races when a painter, by the name of Prust, was knocked down by a horse. The young man received severe injuries and was fortunate that Dr Paddon was quickly able to render assistance.[2]

Other entertainments at the Whitsuntide meeting included old rural sports such as climbing the greasy pole for a new hat, and Cornish and Devon wrestling.

In September 1866 the Swansea and Mumbles Races took place on what was described as 'the new racecourse in

CORNISH AND DEVON WRESTLING

One of the attractions at the Swansea and Blackpill Spring Meeting in 1861 was the 'Cornish and Devon Wrestling', which was won, we are told, by a Cornishman. In fact, there was intense rivalry between the two counties, not least because of the different wrestling styles used either side of the River Tamar. Cornish wrestlers played without shoes, and grasped each other by the short jacket which was always worn. A man could be 'thrust and hugged, and thrown and fallen upon', but kicking in the Devon style was sneered at by the Cornish as being both cruel and unsportsmanlike.

The most famous match of all time took place in 1826 between the Cornish champion James Polinhorne and Abraham Cann of Devon, watched by 8,000 rowdy supporters. There was a fierce dispute over the final verdict, for although Cann was declared the winner, there was no doubt that Polinhorne had lifted his man on high and dashed him to the ground to win the third 'fall'. Eventually the stakes were returned to each party and all bets were declared void.

Rhydydefed Valley, Blackpill,' followed only a month later by the Swansea Races. These were organised by another publican, 'Host Bowen' of the Victoria Hotel, Wind Street. The events were local, if not parochial, in character, with races for ponies, galloways and 'hacks that have not been in public training, and not ridden by professional jockies'. Eight of the nine races over the two meetings were sweepstakes and the September event finished with a real bang – a firework display and a variety of Old English sports.[3]

The next meeting at Rhydydefaid was in October 1870, although several hundred spectators had attended races at Morriston marshes on Easter Monday two years before. The beauty of the Clyne Valley location was often remarked upon but weather ruined the 1870 event. *The Cambrian* waxed lyrical about the event and the weather, reporting that

> The winds roared and wrestled as if they had just escaped from the caves of Aeolus, and the rains descended as if Jupiter Pluvialis had made the necessary arrangements for a local deluge. We often hear of sheet lightning. What would our readers think of sheet rain ?[4]

Things were different the following year when once again Mr Thomas Bullin came to the fore as steward and Clerk of the Course. He joined forces with Mr T Macollum, Managing Director of the London Hippodramatic Fete Company to stage a Hippodramatic Fete on Whit Monday. There were pony, galloway and open races while the other attractions included aeronautic, acrobatic and gymnastic events. It was more like a picnic than a serious race meeting, clearly not what the local press wanted and called for.

A return to the heady days of annual meetings like those held on the Crymlyn Burrows came only after a lapse of a further fifteen years and in autumn 1886 Clyne at last staged a new race meeting. The racetrack was probably in a new location, though it may well have taken in part of the old course, situated as it was about 150 yards south-east of the Rhydydefaid colliery. Surrounded by the oak, elm and ash trees of Clyne and Sketty woods, the meadows must have been a picture.

A committee was appointed, all men of position and character in the community, and planning for the first race meeting began. There was something of a dispute over the timing, the memory of the October 1870 washout being strong enough to give several of the promoters the financial jitters.

In the end the gamble was taken. The races were held that October and as a consequence, Clyne hosted the most successful horse racing the area had seen for thirty years. Between 3,000 and 4,000 people arrived to watch the five races on the card and the Swansea and Mumbles Railway Company even ran special horse cars from the Mumbles Road at Blackpill. The London and North-Western Railway also put on special trains to and from Killay Station. However, in true Swansea race-day tradition many people found their way to the course in brakes, carriages, traps, on the backs of horses and donkeys – and, of course, on foot.

The Swansea and Mumbles Railway was built in 1804 as an industrial tramroad linking the Mumbles with Swansea's network of canals and tramroad feeders. In 1807 the line became unique as the first regular rail passenger service in the world. After periods of financial difficulties and internal wrangling, George Byng Morris restarted the passenger service in 1860 from the Royal Institution to Mumbles, with stops at St Helens and Blackpill.

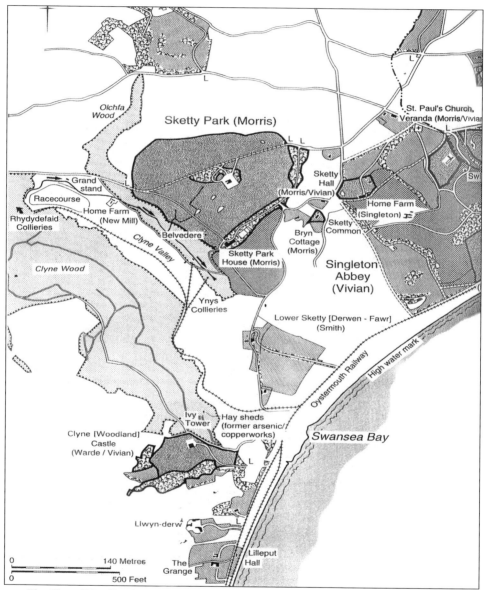

The Clyne Woodlands and Racecourse, portrayed in relation to Sketty Park, and the Oystermouth Railway

(Courtesy as follows: Crown copyright: Royal Commission the Ancient and historical Monuments of Wales)

48

Killay Station, on the London and North-West Railway line

(Courtesy Ray Stock collection)

Bandmaster Davies and the musicians of the Third Glamorgan Rifle Volunteers provided a selection of music as spectators supped many a jug of ale in one of Mr Dowman's refreshment tents. The only gripe, it appears, concerned the siting of the grandstand, which was so badly placed that most spectators could see only a very small proportion of the course.[6]

What was particularly significant about the 1886 meeting at Clyne was that it was a financial success, possibly the first of any of the Swansea races to make a profit. The course itself was not enclosed but nature had provided a natural amphitheatre – it was relatively easy to collect admission fees, as access was limited to certain pathways through the secluded woods. Only Swansea's brigade of determined urchins would have escaped the clutches of the men on the entrances.

The card at the 1886 races consisted of 5 races, including flat, hurdle and pony races as well as two steeplechases. The Penllergare Hunt and Llangyfelach Harriers Steeplechase Plate of £25 was a two-and-a-half mile event covering three laps of the field, one lap being longer than the other two. The obstacles consisted of three banks, a water jump and three flights of hurdles. Riders had to wear the costume of the respective hunts.

Llangyfelach Harriers Hunt c 1904   *(Courtesy Ray Stock collection)*

The profit from the event was used by the committee – people like Colonel Hughes, Mr W. Buckley and the Secretary, Mr J. W. Paradise – to supplement and extend the programme for the races the following June. These fell nicely between the April and August steeplechases at Manselton. On Whit Monday 1888 the 'now popular meeting at Clyne' scored another success but as the races were confined to ponies and galloways, it was, essentially, a local meeting.

Swansea was not renowned as particularly good hunting country, a paucity of foxes compelling local huntsmen to confine their attention to the hare (described as 'puss') As the town grew during the nineteenth century, so the territory available disappeared and they had to widen their scope. According to *The Cambrian* the Llangyfelach Harriers of 1898 would envy their ancestors (The Swansea Harriers) because of the magnificent runs they had during the 1830s :

> . . . not up Pontardawe and Llangafelach, but over the beautiful slopes of the Uplands and the Rhyddings, and right along the top of Town Hill. Their dogs were of a strong breed – a cross between the harrier and the foxhound ; and their mounts were of high mettle. The turnip-field of Glanmor was one of the best places for unearthing puss.

During the 1830s and 40s the Swansea Harriers met twice a week during the season, one meeting point always being Llangyfelach, the other varying between Dunvant Forge, Newton Village, Clyne Common, Three Crosses, Gorseinon and the Black Boy. At the end of the century the pack was small (nine-and-a-half couples) with the curious little dark hound 'Rory' the acknowledged leader. The hunt met on the Neath side on a Tuesday and in Swansea on a Friday, taking in such places as Cilybebyll, Rhydyfro, Clydach, Felindre, Blaenhonddan, Creunant and March Hywel.)

Despite this, there was a large spacious booth in addition to the grandstand and in the evening an Ordinary was held under the presidency of Major Pike.[7]

The 1888 meeting was probably limited to ponies and galloways because of the emergence of the Manselton course the previous year. The Clyne committee seemingly realised that they could not compete with the larger event, which had put Swansea firmly on the horse racing map of Britain and, consequently, took the wise decision not to over-reach itself.

An attempt to transfer the meeting to Manselton in 1889 proved unsuccessful, and the next year the races returned to Clyne. There was a limited field, however, and this time no Ordinary was held. Part of the blame for the distinct lack of success was laid at the door of other races that were taking place across the country that Whit Monday.

By 1893 personnel had changed, and Mr Pond and his energetic committee splashed out to ensure two exciting race-days, both under National Pony and Galloway Rules, one in April, the other in August. Bookmakers came from as far afield as Bristol, entertainment was provided by 'nigger' minstrels, and pickpockets felt it their duty to join in proceedings. However, public support was thin on the ground and when Pond ducked out the following year, G. L. Morris of Sketty took over as Secretary. Whitsun and August Bank Holiday saw some vigorous racing and Sketty Park was thrown open as an extra incentive to ticket holders. At the May event it was reported that the betting men grew angry when objections were lodged against two of the winning horses, one of which was referred to 'head quarters'. Both events held a Manselton Plate (there had been a Manselton Derby in 1893), almost as if the turfites were in denial. Despite a good turnout by the leading local gentry, attendances were becoming poorer and the course 'sloppy in places'.[8] In December Joseph Andrews, jockey, and two local butchers caused mayhem on the

An unknown jockey, with his proud owner, possibly one of the Vivian family, and stable boy
(Courtesy City and County of Swansea: Swansea Museum)

Mumbles road near Singleton grounds when they decided to have a trotting match for £200. Their ponies reached speeds of 14 miles an hour, forcing pedestrians and carriages to veer to the side of the road in panic. They were charged with 'furious driving' and each fined 20s and costs. The following year, 1895, witnessed only an April meeting, when it seems that the bookies almost outnumbered the crowd, though two well-known Clyne runners were amongst the winners at the Wrexham racecourse in August.[9] With attendance even poorer in 1896, the committee resigned and the event floundered.

It was not until 1910 that another race meeting was held at Clyne. *The South Wales Daily Post* of 17th May informed its readers that the trotting, galloping and hurdling races had been revived after a lapse of fifteen years.[10] A huge total of 8,000 spectators came to the meeting, many of them travelling on the Mumbles Railway, which carried over 40,000 passengers on that Bank Holiday alone. The sun shone gloriously, and over £120 was offered in prize money. At 136, the number of entries was so great that several of the six races on the card had to be run in heats.

The programme of events for 1914 showed almost 100 entries, most of them coming from the Swansea and Amman valleys, but then came the Great War and the country had more serious matters on its mind. The revived August Bank Holiday programme in 1924 was, initially, well supported, with over a hundred entries on the card. Dreadful weather

Neath Races took place in September 1927 but the prevalence of foot and mouth disease prevented the attendance of a number of horses entered and backers did not enjoy a good day because in most of the heats there were two joint favourites at very short prices.

The South Wales Daily Post,
September 13th, 1927

conditions, however, reduced the field and no entries came from further east than Cardiff.

Although press reports of the Clyne Valley races at this time are minimal, *The South Wales Daily Post* for 5th August 1924 described the entries as 'quite up to the high standard maintained', thus suggesting that the races were still an annual event.[11] The races may have failed to materialise for the next few years, however, as the same paper talks of horse racing 'recommencing under Welsh Racing Rules' on August Bank Holiday 1927.[12] Numerous improvements were made to the Clyne course at this time, including a reserve paddock and enclosure. It was also rumoured that easier access would be facilitated by the construction of a new road through Sketty Park.

The meeting at Clyne on 15th September 1927 is perhaps most significant for the first appearance in Wales of pony racing under the control of the Pony Turf Club, sanctioned by the Jockey Club. It was highly successful, with stakes amounting to £350 and many entries from over the Welsh border. Races began at 2.15 and went on until 5.30, including events such as The Sketty Plate, The Fairwood Plate, and The Clyne Valley Cup Stakes. A second meeting was held on the first Monday in October, but despite brilliant weather, the course was sodden after heavy weekend rain and the going was heavy. The meeting had been postponed from the previous Thursday and this resulted in poor attendance. There were

Bryn 'Binky' Walker rode the last winner at the Clyne course. He died in June 1984, aged seventy-nine. He began his career at the age of nine and became a successful jockey, riding many winners at courses all over Britain, and picked up a facial disfigurement after being kicked in a 'tumble' during one race. Binky was head ostler with Hancocks, whose brewery was in Little Wind Street and until 1970 drove the Hancock's dray pulled by two beautiful shire horses, Paddy and Laddie.

three plates, the last one resulting in a dead heat between Mr R. J. Everard's Musk Deer and Mr J. Merriman's Our Peggy.

As the crowd drifted away at the end of the day they could not have realised that they had witnessed the final event in the history of racing at Clyne. The reasons for the closure of the racecourse are not clear – it was, after all, a successful venture that attracted enthusiasts from all over Wales. Leonard Jayne, in his book *Pony Racing*, referred to a form book from 1927 that listed pony racing in Sketty Park. A personal friend of Sir T. R. A. Morris, owner of the estate, Jayne commented that, for reasons that nobody really knew, the races simply 'faded out of the picture.'[13]

Postcard of the Clyne Valley Racecourse

(Courtesy Carl Smith collection)

The course itself had something of an indecent burial. After the death of Sir Tankerville Robert Armine Morris in 1930 Swansea Corporation bought the estate and the area was used for landfill. The old racecourse now lies beneath thirty feet of compressed rubbish.

CHAPTER 4

The Rise of Steeplechasing

MOST of the early horse racing at Swansea, either on the Crymlyn Burrows or at Clyne Valley, had been of the 'flat' variety. A hurdle race was held on the Burrows as early as 1837, and thereafter one such race became a regular feature in the annual meetings. As with all hurdle events, however, it was seen simply as a harmless adjunct to the main purpose of flat racing.

A Selling Hurdle Race, similar to those held on the Crymlyn Burrows in the middle of the 19th century : from *The Turf* by A.E.T.Watson, 1898   *(Courtesy the author)*

Hurdling was very different from steeplechasing, even though both involved horses jumping over barriers, and it was only with the advent of the Manselton races at the end of the nineteenth century that the steeplechase finally came to Swansea. In order to place these races into some sort of context, a brief account of the rise of steeplechasing in Britain needs to be made.

The sport of steeplechasing can be traced back to the 'pounding matches' or 'wild goose chases' held in the days of the Tudors when Irish and English horsemen would challenge each other to exhausting contests of skill. One rider would take his own line, as far and as fast as he was able, and the second man would do his best to catch him up. The idea was to 'pound' or 'distance' the second horse.

The first recorded steeplechase was run in County Limerick in 1752, when Mr O'Calloghan and Mr Blake rode from Buttevant Church to St. Mary's, Doneraile, over the same distance (four-and-a-half miles) as a modern Grand National. The earliest matches took place between hunters, owners up, (i.e. ridden by their owners) crossing country from an agreed starting point to a visible object in the distance – a conspicuous church steeple fitting the bill nicely. Fences, ditches and streams had to be crossed in the course of the race. Significantly, the enclosures of the late eighteenth century had transformed the nature of hunting by providing high hedges and wide ditches for horses to clear and before long hunters began to treat the hunting field as a race.

As Roger Munting has said:

> Hunting, with its new thrill of galloping across open country and clearing fences at speed, was as much an influence on the development of steeplechasing as was flat racing.[1]

During the eighteenth century steeplechases were run only occasionally but in 1792 the first recorded cross-country race – as distinct from a two-horse match – took place in Leicestershire. There were no rules and one of the contestants, Lord Forester, was told by a Mr Needham, that he could save 100 yards by coming through his garden and then jumping the gate into the adjacent road![2]

The first regular steeplechase course to be laid out was at Bedford in 1810. At this time owners rode their own horses or put up their friends. One exception to this rule was the daring Dick Christian who was paid for his services. By 1830 three steeplechase courses were listed and it was in this year that Thomas Coleman initiated the St Albans steeplechase. This event established steeplechase racing on a regular basis, rather than the spasmodic, unorganised affair that it had previously been.

The St Albans Steeplechase   *(Courtesy the author)*

Coleman was a publican and an entrepreneur who looked upon the St Albans races as a commercial venture. He had to recompense local farmers whose land was churned up by the horses and riders – and he did so through the copious supply of wines and spirits. Although the St Albans steeplechase declined in popularity within eight years, it sparked off a growth in the sport in many other parts of Britain. Between 1830 and 1838 the number of meetings increased from just three to thirty-nine. These included events at Haverfordwest (1834) and Abergavenny (1838). By 1842 there were sixty-six steeplechase meetings, often arranged by hunt members or by farmers themselves and with races taking place over wide stretches of countryside that had been marked out by flags.

Another publican, William Lynn of the Waterloo Hotel, Aintree, established the "Grand Liverpool Steeplechase" in 1836. Although most of the race was run over open country and natural fences, part of it took place on his Aintree flat course – the Grand National (although still then known as the Grand Liverpool) had been born.

Although steeplechasing bore all the traits of the fox hunting scene, the latter preserved an air of social exclusiveness that steeplechasing did not attempt to imitate. Indeed, during the first half of the nineteenth century there was violent opposition to the sport from hunting, humanitarian and moral lobbies. Many members of the hunting fraternity were reluctant to bring any form of racing into hunting country. The gentry found themselves repelled by the steeplechase crowds which Nimrod, an influential voice in hunting circles, described as 'ignorant townsmen and ignorant legs.'[3]

Due to the dangers to both horses and riders, many thought steeplechasing a cruel sport. *The Liverpool Mercury* even put the first Grand National on a par with cockfighting and bull-baiting, remarking that '. . . we can no more be reconciled to it . . . than we are to cockfighting, bull-baiting, or any other popular *pastime* which is intended with the infliction of wanton torture to any living being.'[4]

The middle-class crusade against 'cruel' sports included steeplechasing on its hit list. Hunting and shooting were protected because they were the preserves of the rich, while flat racing could count on noble and royal patronage. However, steeplechasing escaped the wrath of the more vehement moral crusaders because it was a rural and occasional event in most districts and was even proposed as a substitute for bullbaiting in Ashbourne, Derbyshire.[5]

There was an undoubted 'snob' lobby against steeplechasing in these years, people like the witty novelist Robert Surtees who declared that such events were a generally crude and badly arranged farce. They had, he said, not the wild excitement of the hunt, nor the accurate calculating quality of the racecourse.[6]

Despite the opposition, steeplechasing continued to thrive and gain in popularity. However, standards continued to deteriorate and genuine supporters of the sport believed that a judicial tribunal to govern and regulate steeplechasing was an urgent necessity. When the Grand National Hunt Committee was formed in 1863 it was significant that one of its members was Mr W G Craven, a member of the Jockey Club, and that Admiral Rous gave assistance in the formulation of their

> **SURTEES ON STEEPLECHASING –**
>
> *. . . Few sportsmen will act as Stewards a second time; while the victim to the popular delusion of patronising our 'national sports' considers – like gentlemen who have served the office of sheriff or churchwarden – that once in a lifetime is enough; hence there is always the air of amateur actorship about them. Either they forget the ropes, or they forget the scales, or they forget the bell, or – more commonly still – some of the parties forget themselves . . .*
>
> *Plain or Ringlets,*
> by R.S. Surtees, 1860

rules. Three years later the Jockey Club gave its blessing to the formation of the Grand National Steeplechase Committee, even though there were, as yet, no formal links between the two bodies. In 1867 the Committee adopted hurdle racing by default when the Jockey Club decided that such races should no longer be governed by their rules.

Although the number of minor meetings increased, the 1850s was actually seen as a period of declining standards. The events were often organised by publicans to boost their trade and before long there were too many meetings for the number of horses available. Clerks of Courses made fences too easy and weights too low in order to attract big fields. Because the Jockey Club refused to recognise steeplechasing, a jockey or trainer could get up to all sorts of tricks, which would have been regarded as blatant misconduct at a flat-racing event. Lord Suffolk described the sport as 'the recognised refuge of all outcasts, human and equine, from the legitimate turf.'

Admiral Rous was first elected a Steward of the Jockey Club in 1838 and by a process of continuous re-election, emerged as 'Dictator of the Turf' in the early 1860s. He published the revolutionary 'Weight For Age Scale' in his *Laws and Practice of Horse Racing* in 1850, based on twelve years study and revised it in 1873.

By the end of the 1860s the Grand National Hunt Steeplechase Committee was accepted as the ruling body of steeplechasing, its members rapidly gaining in confidence. During the next two decades the Committee slowly perfected its own organisation, one of the biggest problems being how to stamp its authority on all steeplechase meetings. It published its own calendar for steeplechasing and hurdling, the first 'Weatherby's Steeplechase

Calendar' being dated 1866 – 1867. Regulations regarding fences and the number and type of obstacles had to be worked out in detail. A sub-committee report in 1882 argued that the principal cause of the decline that had hit steeplechasing after 1876 was the diminution in the size, number and variety of fences. It recommended that in every steeplechase course of two miles there should be at least twelve fences, that each course should have a water jump measuring 12 foot wide by 6 foot deep, and that every mile should have an open ditch, 6 foot wide and 4 foot deep on the taking-off side. Uniformity not only reinforced the authority of the Committee and ensured the likelihood of a true contest, but was also essential for safety reasons.

Some of the jockeys who had appeared at the Swansea Races were celebrated Grand National figures, moving from one code to another when plagued by increasing weight and tending to ride only over hurdles at flat-race meetings. One such was William Archer who rode Master Frederick to victory in the 1855 Hurdle Race at the Burrows. He rode in several Grand Nationals, coming second in 1854 and winning on Little Charley in 1858.

Tommy Pickernell, alias the outstanding 'Mr Thomas', an experienced and respected Grand National jockey, three times winner of the Grand National (1860,1871 and 1875). He was appointed Inspector of National Hunt courses in 1884 : *A Race Apart*, Reg Green, Hodder & Stoughton, 1988

(Courtesy Reg Green)

The report reflected the sharp division that existed amongst 'chase' followers. One party believed that steeplechasing should be testing and contested by big, safe jumpers of the hunter variety. Others considered that thoroughbred horses flipping over 'park' fences would be less dangerous to men and animals alike. Those yearning for a return to the natural obstacles of the hunting field could not, it seems, come to terms with the more sophisticated requirements of a growing entertainment business.

Between 1866 and 1886 the number of steeplechase meetings increased from eighty-nine to one hundred and seventy-five. The vast majority of these were once-a-year events that took place in and around the major urban centres. The sport was learning to survive by adapting, as and when necessary. Throughout the nineteenth century gradual links were made with the world of flat racing, its association with hunting becoming a thing of the past.

The period from 1870 to 1914 witnessed profound changes in the pattern of leisure activities as working hours were reduced and a real upward trend in working-class wages took place. Steeplechasing moved with the times. It became more businesslike. Specialised tasks within the sport began to emerge – trainers, jockeys and so on – and the working people of Britain discovered that here, indeed, was a sport they could enjoy and, if they wanted, patronise with their money.

CHAPTER 5

Manselton – Success!

O N Christmas Eve 1886 a small advertisement appeared in *The Cambrian* newspaper. It must have sent a shiver of excitement through all 'turfites' in the area, rekindling many happy memories for those old enough to remember the glory days of the Crymlyn Burrows Races. According to the advertisement, a new racecourse was to be laid out at Manselton (or Mansel Town as it was sometimes known) on land belonging to Richard Mansel Mansel. The Swansea and South Wales Races would be held there, under Grand National Hunt Rules, on Easter Monday and Tuesday 1887.[1]

Swansea already had tenuous links with steeplechasing. There had been hurdle races at the Burrows and a tentative proposal to establish steeplechases in the town in 1847. At Clyne, the successful 1886 meeting included two proper steeplechases – perhaps as a result of the rumour that there was soon to be an official steeplechase course at Manselton.

The driving force behind the Manselton enterprise was a man by the name of Arthur Burr. Described as a financial agent, he was the epitome of the shady Victorian speculator, and his business partner in the Manselton racecourse was one Frederick Lovell Keays. It seems certain that Burr manoeuvred himself into the ideal position to persuade the reckless young Richard Mansel Mansel to finance the racecourse on his land and to dupe Arthur Chichester Burnard, agent to the Manselton Estate.

The Mansel family owned extensive estates in South Wales but when Richard Mansel Mansel inherited these under the terms of his father's will, dated 1875, he became only 'tenant for life'. It meant that he could enjoy the income from the estates but could not sell any of them. Unlike his careful and attentive father and grandfather before him, young Richard promptly proceeded to squander his assets. Like many a titled gentleman, he was a gambler devoted to horse racing and he frittered away a fortune.

It is significant that the first race meeting at Manselton took place in April 1887. Shortly before that date Arthur Burr had an appeal to recoup the sum of £1,200 from the Mansel estate turned down by Lords Justices Cotton, Lindley and Lopes.[2] What the debt was for remains unknown but, away from the court where he was protected by solicitors and trustees, Mansel was vulnerable to a predator like Burr. It is quite possible that Burr negotiated a private deal with Mansel in order to regain the money he was owed, perhaps a future share of the finished racecourse being the carrot needed to ensure co-operation.

The course at Manselton was more akin to a modern racecourse than to the Crymlyn which, though only redundant for quarter of a century, was now being consigned to a period of racing history rapidly becoming outdated. The course itself was a wonderful affair – 'a right-handed one, of an elliptical formation and laid out for flat,

The Mansel Coat of Arms, granted to the 1st Baronet in 1621. The motto reads *Quod vult valde vult:* 'What he wishes, he wishes fervently'
(Courtesy Sir Philip Mansel, Bart)

flying and banking races, measuring about a mile-and-a-half round, and scientifically constructed according to the rules of the Grand National Committee, with privet quick and gorse banks, open, ditch and water jump.'[3]

A major break with the past was the fact that Manselton was an enclosed course, one of many that had sprung up in Britain since 1875. The course consisted of 140 acres, the enclosure alone being 97 acres in size. At the Swansea entrance it was soon deemed necessary to double the number of turnstiles from seven to fourteen, in order to facilitate easier access. On the Landore side there were eighteen turnstiles by the time of the second meeting, while the carriage entrance, with its large swing gates supported by massive oak pillars, was an impressive sight. Mansel arranged for the oak fences to be produced and sent down from the Lingfield Estate where he spent much of his time.

Construction of the course had been something of a local wonder. What had been a virtual marsh was turned into a perfect grass course, much of it laid down to Suttons' 'celebrated lawn seed'. A system of innumerable pipes drained off all surface water.

The Turnstiles at Manselton:
(from *The Illustrated Sporting and Dramatic News*, August 13th, 1887)
(Courtesy WJ)

The Carriage Entrance:
(from *The Illustrated Sporting and Dramatic News*, August 13th, 1887)
(Courtesy WJ)

Throughout the hot summer of 1887 carts could be seen day and night, trundling back and forth between the new course and Bevan's Farm which lay to the west, bringing water to keep the turf in peak condition. An old coal pit that used to exist near the new grandstand was filled in and the black hoarding around it – offensive to the eye – was removed. The approach to the Swansea entrance was tastefully laid out with trees, shrubs and flowers enclosed by brown iron fences with barbs painted, alternately, in blue and gold. Young trees and shrubs adorned the south side of the course while, at the western end, an ornamental bank of rhododendrons had been planted.[4]

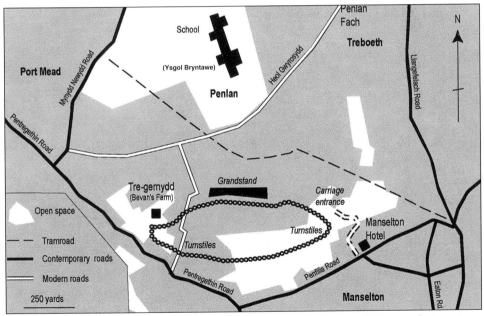

The layout of the Manselton Racecourse in what is now Penlan, in relation to modern-day roads and buildings, based on all the available evidence. It shows the position of the course itself, together with the turnstiles and the carriage entrance. Bevan's Farm, the source of the irrigation supply, can be seen to the west of the course.

(Courtesy Tim Fearnside FBCartS)

The atmosphere of the first meeting in April 1887 can only be described as festive. Large numbers of people from all the neighbouring counties flocked to the track and were rewarded by glorious sunshine and some good racing. There were between 30,000 and 50,000 spectators on the first day alone and while the second day, a Tuesday and not, therefore, a Bank Holiday, was not so well attended, it seemed that an auspicious start to the enterprise had been made.

The course was ideally situated for easy access, particularly with regard to railway travel. Visitors from Hereford or Brecon who used the Midland Railway could alight at Morriston, just one-and-a-half miles away. A mile away in the other direction lay the Great Western's station at High Street, while anyone travelling on the

TRANSPORT TO THE RACES

'At that first historic meeting, all sorts of vehicles were engaged, including the tramcars which were jam packed. Mr Sugrue, manager of the Tramways Company, had stationed himself for the afternoon near the site of the projected Pavilion Music Hall in High Street, and from the point of vantage he directed the traffic 'as a captain navigates a ship standing on the bridge.' The heavy load of the crowded cars was mastered by an attachment of an extra horse, the appearance of the three horses abreast suggestive of the pictures of Russian vehicular traffic. Several four-in-hand brakes attracted attention, especially those of Messrs Bullin, Rosser and Major Pike. But at the other end of the scale there were some ramshackle old carriages, which looked like the resurrections of fifty years ago.'

The Cambrian congratulated the Tramways Company on the fact that despite transporting a large portion of the 50,000 spectators on Easter Monday and Tuesday 1887, 'no accident of any nature occurred to mar the proceedings'. This wasn't quite true, however, as in October William Lewis, a tin-plate worker from Pontardulais, brought an action against the company for injuries received at the end of the first day of the races, and was awarded £50 damages. In boarding one of the trams at Cwmbwrla, he had mounted to the top and put his hand on the handrail which was loose. He had fallen over into the road, suffering bad injuries to his back and head which had kept him off work for four months.

(The Cambrian 15-4-1887, 28-10-1887)

London and North Western Line would disembark at Swansea Bay station, some three miles distant. Interestingly, a notice in the advertisement columns of *The Cambrian*, signed by Captain Colquhoun, Head Constable, gave warning that no hackney carriages would be allowed to ply for hire within the Borough unless they had previously been licensed for the purpose.[5] John Prosser of Oxford Street and David Jones of Brynhyfryd thought the risk worth taking but were caught out by Sergeant Davies, inspector of cabs. Prosser's defence was that his one-horse wagonette had been hailed in High Street by a few of his friends wanting to go to the races. The magistrates came down on the side of the licensed cabman who had shopped him, however, and fined him 13/6d for his troubles.[6] For others, no doubt, cashing in on the success of the Manselton races paid off.

A fine course and a beautiful setting were not in themselves enough to ensure success. If a spectator was to be persuaded to part with his money at the gate, then the course also had to offer him something special once he was inside the ground. To this end the facilities at Manselton ensured that it was a thoroughly modern affair.

The grandstand could accommodate 2,500 people and was described as an elegant structure of great strength, erected on piles that had been driven deeply into the rock.[7] The frontage was laid out in sloping concrete, a mound having been levelled out by around five feet, thus adding to the view. At some stage in the future, it was said, a cricket pitch would be laid out on this spot. From the stand, spectators could see every part of the course. During the races, betting transactions went on freely within the grandstand, it had every conceivable convenience, and 'the good old institutions of

The Grandstand (from *The Illustrated Sporting and Dramatic News*, August 13th, 1887)

The grandstand had been designed by architect Mr Buckley Wilson RIBA. During the early part of the year he had been doing some work on the old Cross Keys tavern, the site of the fourteenth-century Hospital of the Blessed David. According to *The Cambrian* he had done much to recover the form and fashion of the old Hospital.

(CourtesyWJ)

eating and drinking flourished'. The kitchens, which formed an annex of the grandstand, were made of brick and stone. The whole structure was built at a cost of £6,300.

To the east of the grandstand lay the paddock. It had stables and every modern appliance, including its own telegraph office. The General Post Office always sent a special corps of turf telegraphists to race meetings across the country and it was to these experts that the public was indebted for their evening-paper reports and race results.

The existence of a private stand, a county stand, carriage enclosures and the magnificent grandstand itself, would seem to indicate that the course had its own club. *The Cambrian* confirms that at the second meeting, which took place in August 1887, there was a particularly large contingent of handsome and well-dressed ladies, their role being – according to the paper – 'to lend charm to the scene.'[8] Indeed, in the bid to attract spectators to enclosed courses, two groups attained new significance, ladies and the working class.

It cost one shilling for the ordinary punter to gain admission to the Manselton course. It was the basic entrance fee to most enclosed racecourses at this time (soccer was relatively cheap at 6d.), a sum that was 'within the pocket of sufficient working men to satisfy the course management.'[9] With the establishment of the Saturday half-day it made sense for racecourses to offer Saturday afternoon racing. Steeplechasing, however, was only an occasional event in most areas, with Whit Monday being a particularly popular date. At Manselton, four of the five major meetings held there between April 1887 and June 1889 were held on Bank Holidays. People were in a holiday mood and a day at the races, starting at 1.30pm, would continue well into the evening and offer plenty of excitement and entertainment.

If the excitement engendered at steeplechase meetings is measured by the number of horses that fell at the fences, then there certainly seemed to be plenty of it. During the April 1887 meeting St David injured himself severely when he refused the first fence during the Hunters' Steeplechase and attempted to jump it from the railings.[10]

The Landore Hunters Hurdle Race, The Last Flight : (from *The Illustrated Sporting and Dramatic News*, April 23rd, 1887)

To the left of our view of the grandstand is the ground laid out for shows and beer tents: on the other side of the main stand stood the private stands, paddock and enclosure. At the beginning of the nineteenth century the classes had mixed freely, but by now the 'riff-raff' were segregated from the genteel racegoers. Notice the spectators outside the ground, on their vantage point behind the grandstand.

(Courtesy WJ)

Two horses fell during the August Bank Holiday event, followed by four at the Christmas meeting, two of them in the same race.[11] In October 1888 Captain Lindsay's Rosebery had to be shot after falling and dislocating a shoulder in The Singleton Steeplechase, the luckless owner falling again in the Open Steeplechase later in the day. In the Tradesmen's Plate Taffina fell, while Foul Play threw its jockey after refusing a fence.[12]

Gambling, of course, was an integral part of a day at the races and betting at the Manselton course was as brisk as anywhere else –

> Bookmakers rigged out in extraordinary habiliments, mounted their boxes and clamoured 'Four to one, bar one,' 'Six to one, bar three,' and took money, paid money and eyed the course with a rapidity borne of long practice and a coolness that it would take many years of patient study to acquire.[13]

One racegoer, 'Pierre Claire', who was stitched up by the bookies, put pen to paper and wrote an amusing, self-deprecating poem to *The Cambrian* entitled 'The Welshman At The Races'. Realising his naivety in believing that his winnings would be posted to his home address, he eagerly anticipated what was to come on the domestic front:

> With regard to the cash
> Which I hope it will come,
> As I spent rather rash
> And am still on the roam;
> For my wife got good bit of a temper,
> And I'm 'fraid in my heart to go home.[14]

It wasn't just the bookies, however, who were intent on making money at the races. Harriett Crabtree of the Apple Tree Inn was fined 12s for selling liquor on the racecourse without a license,[15] while gaming tables were in evidence and 'professors of the three-card trick and other species of social larceny worked themselves up into proper business condition.'[16] Many people undoubtedly got caught and the mounted police that protected the course were kept busy. Led by Captain Colquhoun, Superintendents Hollet, Howlet and others, they were reported as keeping 'perfect order' at the Christmas meeting on Boxing Day 1887.[17]

It was also common practice for plain-clothes policemen to attend race meetings, acting independently of the local force. These men knew all the regular villains of the turf and were highly efficient in arresting criminals. Benjamin Wood of Bristol, for example, was sentenced to six weeks' hard labour at Swansea Police Court for stealing a gentleman's opera glasses at the August 1887 meeting. Francis Farrel of Manchester received two months with hard labour for relieving a

THE SCAMPS ON THE RACECOURSE

At the very first Manselton meeting, six men from Cardiff, Merthyr, Plymouth and Swansea were charged with gambling, and evidence against them given not only by Detective Morris of Swansea, but by detectives from Scotland Yard, Birmingham and Bristol.

There is no doubt that these petty criminals brought a lot of colour to the race scene. Take George Thompson of Cardiff, for example, who was caught playing a game of tombola with the crowd. When charged, he had made £10, pocketing between 2s and 4s every time he swivelled his cylindrical box. As he stood upon a stool with a table in front of him, a monkey sitting on his shoulder would watch him deal out the tin tickets and on cue from his master, pull one of the numbered balls out of the container.

At the Boxing day meeting, William Stewart was fined £1 for playing a game of chance called 'over and under the seven' with a box and dice. His defence was that he had played it before the Prince of Wales and that it was, therefore, perfectly legal !

Swansea man, William Jenkins, of a sovereign by means of the three-card trick. Robert Marsden of Liverpool, charged with playing a game of chance on the course, was discharged on promising to depart Swansea sooner rather than later.[18]

The atmosphere at the Manselton Races must have been vibrant, to say the least. Booths, shows and other objects of amusement were provided for the general public, fifteen beer tents at the Christmas meet alone – 'From some came the sounds of musical instruments, and now and then, of singing, which showed that the people were having a fairly good time of it.'[19]

As with the earlier races on the Crymlyn Burrows there would have been a lot of Welsh spoken. The areas immediately surrounding the racecourse were all Welsh-speaking, much of Glamorgan had not yet been anglicised, and the

---

DRINKING BOOTHS

Although we do not have a detailed description of the atmosphere inside one of those beer tents, it must have been very similar to one of the large, busy drinking booths at Llangyfelach Fair, visited by a reporter in March 1891 :

> . . . It is filled with men and women, young and old, whose features are almost blackened with the smoke which fills the place. A glance at the faces of some present tell a tale of reckless dissipation. See yon young fellow . . . He is a loafer, a sharper and a rogue. See how glibly he talks with the intoxicated young yokel. He is up to some dodge, I wager. Pass on to the other end of the tent ; here are a few town women and men, fairly well dressed, but who lead what is termed a 'loose life.' They are red with port, and redolent of slang. Close by sit three or four young fellows drinking and smoking, and their talk is of a drink, women, and betting . . .

Norman Lewis Thomas in *The Story of Swansea's Districts and Villages*, quotes Mr John Davies, a retired master builder, who was born in July 1884 recalling in some detail life in Cwmbwrla and Fforestfach: '. . . At about 5 years of age I went to Cwmbwrla Infants' School, where I heard English spoken for the first time, but only by the teachers. The children from Cwmbwrla, Manselton and Gendros all spoke Welsh . . .'

visitors travelling from West Wales would almost certainly have spoken Welsh.

The Manselton still stands on Penfilia Road. It once provided accommodation for guests attending the nearby races

(Courtesy the author)

The Manselton was built as a private hotel in 1886 by Sir Richard Mansel Mansel specifically to house guests and the jockeys who had travelled from all over the British Isles to attend the race meetings. The new hotel however did not find favour with all sections of the Swansea population. A local temperance mob, presumably under instructions from God, broke into the cellars, hauled up the smaller barrels of beer and rolled them down Manor Road, where they smashed at the bottom of the hill![20]

Such an incident may well have led to attempts to appease the Evangelists. A reporter from *The Cambrian* noticed several coffee taverns on the grounds at the April meeting. How many customers they served we can only speculate upon, but the Swansea Coffee Public House Movement claimed to have supplied 400,000 persons with refreshment at its five houses in 1881.

The coffee temperance booth would have resembled this gospel tent, seen here with its organizing committee.

(Courtesy City and County of Swansea: Swansea Museum)

An advertisement for the Christmas Race Meeting 1887 invited tenders for the supply of refreshments not only to the grandstand and show ground, but also to a 'coffee temperance booth'. Some notable civic figures had signed the pledge, there was a range of anti-drink societies and organisations in the town, and *The Cambrian* was at pains to point out that the whole Manselton race scheme had been organised 'solely in the interest of sport as sport, and not in any way as a degenerating influence.'

A RESPECTABLE PUBLIC HOUSE

By making a drinking establishment the headquarters of the races, Sir Richard was following in good steeplechasing tradition. The fact that the Swansea Licensed Victuallers Association sponsored each of the Manselton meetings with some form of plate is proof that to some extent the publicans regarded the race meeting as 'their' event. This would have given an extra edge to the remarkable hostility that existed between the brewing trade and the temperance societies in Swansea at this time. Open-air protest meetings were held by the local religious denominations near the hotel, which had virtually become a Sunday drinking club run by the Unionist Association after the failure of the racecourse. Attempts by the owners to apply for a six days' licence, which would have rid the district of the disorderly scenes on the Sabbath, were opposed by the Temperance Party at the annual Brewster Sessions year after year. They wanted neither the greater nor the lesser evil. The hotel was at last granted a licence in 1894 and could set about the task of becoming a respectable public house.

The New Race : symbol of a new racecourse, and a new enterprise in an industrial landscape (from *The Illustrated Sporting and Dramatic News,* April 23rd, 1887)

(Courtesy WJ)

After the success of the inaugural meeting it seemed as if Manselton would soon become an important part of the racing scene. The basic entrance fee of one shilling was paid by 25,000 spectators who passed through the turnstiles. On top of this, many were admitted by tickets of 5s or 10s giving entrance to the grandstand and private stands while it would be an extra 5s for the privilege of looking over the runners in the paddock. One, two and four-horse carriages were admitted at the rate of 5s, 10s and £1 respectively, while a reserved carriage enclosure would cost another 5s.[21] Mansel, Arthur Burr and their associates must have been rubbing their hands together in expectation. And then came the crash!

CHAPTER 6

Manselton – Failure

Had the Manselton venture succeeded it may well have kept the profligate Richard Mansel Mansel afloat for a little while longer. Yet within two years the project was in total disarray and, by 1891, the Bankruptcy Court in London was examining the affairs of Arthur Burr.

MR ARTHUR BURR'S AFFAIRS

The Cambrian, and presumably its readers, took a continued interest in Arthur Burr's demise, reporting as it did throughout the latter part of 1891 the proceedings of the bankruptcy case against him :

> ... It appears that the debtor commenced business in 1880 as a land agent, that ... since 1885 he has been engaged in financing the Bellagio estate; and also in the purchase of freehold estates and interests, and in the construction of racecourses at Lingfield and Swansea ... He had also financed Sir Richard Mansel, whose affairs were brought into the court about 1883. He estimated that he had paid about £30,000 on account of losses in connection with the Swansea racecourse scheme, and was liable for £20,000 more ... An altercation took place between Mr Burr and Mr Beyfus, representing the trustee of Sir Richard Mansel's estate, and in the result the examination was ordered to be concluded ...

> *The Cambrian*, November 20th, 1891

On the face of it there was every reason for it to succeed. The course itself was a model of modern sporting arenas, ideally set to become a centre for racing in South West Wales. The men who formed the executive were mainly businessmen from England, together with a sprinkling of local dignitaries. Lord Tredegar of Monmouthshire figured prominently in the Christmas meeting while two of the stewards in 1887, Colonel F C Morgan, MP, and W H P Jenkins, were senior figures in the steeplechasing world.

There were many other factors in favour of the enterprise succeeding. Swansea had a hundred-year-old tradition of horse racing, firstly on the Crymlyn Burrows and then at Clyne. There was obviously a solid core of 'turfites' who would support racing in the area.

Several hunts across South and West Wales had held successful steeplechase meetings for a number of years. Tenby, Carmarthen and Abergavenny hosted such events almost continuously from 1870 until the end of the century, as did Cardiff for many years. It would have been realistic to assume that these hunts and their followers would support well-organised steeplechase meetings in the Swansea area.

Steeplechasing was a growing business towards the end of the Victorian era, unlike flat racing which lost 89 meetings from the Racing Calendar in the last quarter of the century.[1] Prize-money regulations in steeplechasing were less exacting, £20 being the minimum per race as compared to £100 guarantee for the winner on the flat – a factor that pushed many courses towards National Hunt racing.

Gate-money sport had already become popular in Swansea. Between 1870 and 1900 rugby developed into a mass spectator-sport in South Wales, some 8,000 crowding into the St Helen's stadium to watch the Swansea v Cardiff game in the 1886-7 season. The gate-money of £113 was reported to have been the largest ever taken locally. A few years later 7,000 people paid their entrance fees at the same venue to watch Wales take on Ireland at soccer.[2] The economic boom then taking place in South Wales ensured that the working classes generally had sufficient income to support some sort of leisure activity.

With admission money, the sale of numerous refreshment and showground plots and the money derived from selling races, the Manselton Races should have been financially secure. Selling races were a particularly lucrative way of raising funds, entry conditions for such races declaring that the winner had to be sold for a certain sum. Of the thirty-one races run at the four steeplechase meetings in 1887 and 1888, selling races accounted for nine of them. The difference between the auction price and the nominated selling price was divided equally between the race fund and the second horse. For example, after the South Wales Selling Hunters' Steeplechase had been run on the second day of the Easter meeting 1887, Ulster Chief was sold by auction to a Mr Walton for 125 guineas. This gave a surplus to the race fund of £31 5s over the 100 sovereigns nominated selling price. Lord Suffolk, a Jockey Club steward, writing in *Badminton Magazine* in May 1888, maintained that 'selling races as at present carried on are the vital principle of most meetings, for they constitute an unfailing source of revenue.'[3]

> ## REFRESHMENT BOOTHS
>
> At the August Bank Holiday Meeting 1887, fifteen plots were set apart for refreshment booths adjoining the grandstand, each with a frontage of 30 feet. In addition there was a plot of ground 'for the absolute right of selling tea, coffee, and non-intoxicating drinks'. These plots were sold by auction at the Mackworth Arms Hotel two weeks before the races. In addition, the proprietors of the racecourse reserved the right to erect a marquee on the enclosed ground at the back of the grandstand for the sale of refreshments exclusively to those who paid admission to the grandstand or paddock.

So what went wrong? Certainly all the excitement and local interest surrounding the establishment of the racecourse and the race meetings was substantial. Yet it disguised the sad fact that the venture was far too ambitious. The initial capital outlay needed to create what must have been one of the most beautiful courses in Britain, with all its accoutrements and support mechanisms, would

---

RICHARD MANSEL MANSEL IS DECLARED BANKRUPT

Many titled gentlemen were ruined by gambling. As a young man in his twenties Mansel married the beautiful 17-year-old Maud Margaretta Bowen, youngest daughter of John Jones of Maes-y-crugiau, Carmarthenshire. He built a large country house for her on the Lingfield Estate and during the period 1875 – 1883 raised three mortgages on his inheritance which amounted to £33,000. His failure to pay some items of income from estate rentals that were to be paid to his sisters and surviving brothers under his father's will led to the beneficiaries taking him to a whole series of court cases in the High Court of Chancery. Living off his reputation, he went to America, from where he despatched notes to the Trustees of the Swansea estates requesting more money to feed his gambling habit. By 1883 the Trustees of the Wimbledon Estate had taken him to court and applied for liquidation with the result that the Land Agent was given the power to run the estate.

When he appeared in the Court of Bankruptcy his address was given as the Army and Navy Hotel, Westminster and he stated that he had stayed at various hotels since 1878. Presumably this period was one long gambling binge, for he also affirmed that Lady Mansel had private property and that it was she who paid the hotel bills! By 1885 she had drunk herself to death and he used her assets to avoid bankruptcy, negotiating his liabilities by selling the silver plate, jewellery, china and books that she had left to her family. In about 1886 he had even tried his hand at managing the Empire Theatre in Leicester Square, even though he had no capital, relying on a certain Major Newitt and Mr David Nicholls to put up the money. In a short period they managed to make a substantial loss on a pantomime and a production of 'Round the World in Sixty Days.' The lessor of the Theatre had brought an action against Mansel.

In 1887 Mansel was sued for defaults on two mortgages and in one final case at the High Court of Justice on August 9th, 1888 before Justice Chitty, he was declared bankrupt. Arthur Burr was among his creditors. Mansel soldiered on with his profligate lifestyle by marrying music-hall entertainer Ada Alice in 1891 who in July of that year (and now Lady Mansel) was performing at the Trocadero Music Hall for £40 a week.

---

have been enormous. While there is no clear proof, it is more than probable that the Executive Committee was relying on the promise of capital from Arthur Burr, capital that he could not realistically raise – there was only so much that he could squeeze out of the gullible Richard Mansel.

Simply to construct the course would have involved dozens of different companies, people like Messrs Thomas, Watkins and Jenkins who built the grandstand, Captain Sumner who laid out and built a new road at the Landore entrance and Mr Barron of Sketty who planted all the trees and shrubs. Each of these, and many more, needed to be paid for their labour. Extra land had to be purchased from Richard Richards in order to make the park at the rear of the grandstand. It all cost money.

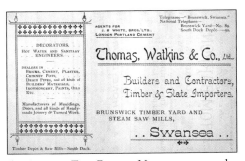

Letter headings for two of the Swansea businesses, Tom Barron, Nurseryman, and Messrs Thomas, Watkins & Co. Ltd, Builders, which were actively concerned with the construction of the Manselton Racecourse

(Courtesy Swansea Reference Library)

Staging the races would also have been very costly. In order to attract good quality entries the Executive offered to refund the railway fares from any station in England or Wales, as well as boat fares from Waterford, Dublin or Cork, of all horses running at the track. Fifty loose boxes were made available on the ground, with hay and straw provided free of charge, while Pwll-y-domen farm, adjoining the course, was converted into stables by Mansel with excellent sleeping chambers for the stable lads.[4] Such facilities may well have attracted owners but they were also very costly.

Despite the huge expenses, gate receipts on the first meeting in April 1887 would have netted in excess of £2,000 and it is quite possible that, when solicited contributions, booth rents, stand fees

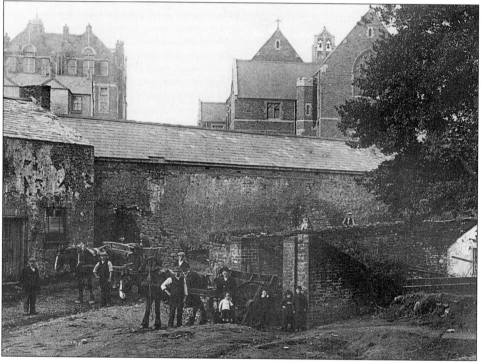

View of Pwll-y-domen Farm,

The stables were called the Millward Stables and stood on the old medieval road (where the Manor Cinema site is in Bohun Street, Manselton) leading to Pentregethin Road, which was the main route to Carmarthen. The stables were later taken over by Joslin who did large amounts of haulage work for the G.W.R., ran a regular service to the Gower and provided horses for the army.

(Courtesy Colin Bevan)

and money from selling races were added, these first April races made some sort of profit.

The Cambrian, as was to be expected, gave unconditional support to any new enterprise in the area and was positive in its assessment of the meeting. However, even its enthusiastic reporting of the event could not disguise the fact that something was amiss. Entries to races were disappointing. Two of the most attractive items in the first day's racing were substituted by 'walk overs', in which, for one reason or another, there was only one runner in the race, and where that horse was simply required to 'walk over' the course to win the prize. Two of the second day's races were declared void, including the Cambrian Hunters' Open Hurdle, for which thirteen runners had originally been entered. Receipt of entry fees – typically three sovereigns for a £100 prize, one or two sovereigns for a lesser one – would have been meagre. In an attempt to redress the situation the Committee literally 'upped the stakes' for the second meeting, offering prize money of 930 sovereigns for only six races on that August Monday, doubling the value of what had been on offer in April.

Prince Charles Kinsky

The celebrated Jockey, whose horse St Galmier competed at the April 1887 meeting. Portrait in *Heroes and Heroines of the Grand National*, Finch Mason, 1911

(Courtesy York Racing Museum and Library)

The Jubilee Hunters' Steeplechase: Count Kimsky's St Galmier (from *The Illustrated Sporting and Dramatic News,* April 23rd, 1887)

The Jubilee Hunters Staple Chase
Count Kinskys St Galmier
W. O.

The fact that one of Count Kinsky's horses was to run in the races would have attracted many punters to Manselton, especially if the rumour had got about that the Prince himself was to be present. An Austro-Hungarian magnate, Count Charles Kinsky became the first 'foreigner' to win the Grand National, when he rode his favourite mare Zoedone to victory in 1883. St Galmier was a full brother to Zoedone and had been the winner of 8 races from 9 starts in 1887, including the Liverpool Hunt Steeplechase at the Grand National. Perhaps other owners were afraid to pit their horses against him, the clear 'W. O.' on the print signifying a 'walkover'. The crowd were particularly disappointed at not being able to witness St Galmier in full flow.

(Courtesy WJ)

The racing at the second meeting proved to be far better than on the first occasion, with each race, apart from the opening one, attracting a field of between seven and ten horses. However, the attendance was substantially down –'It is true that the grandstand and the county stand were pretty nearly filled and the paddock realised a considerable sum of money by the number of its visitors. But the general public did not turn up in such force.'[5]

The Executive Committee had managed to attract a bigger field by offering more substantial prize money and those who turned up undoubtedly had an enjoyable day. However, the enclosed gate-money course at Manselton probably had to rely on a crowd of between ten and twenty-thousand in order to prosper. The required number simply did not come.

That year had already seen successful meetings at places like Carmarthen, Pembroke and Cardiff. After April, the only scheduled meeting for the year in South Wales was at Caerleon, so it could be reasonably assumed that an August meeting would have been something of a novelty and well patronised by the general public.

Possibly the organisers were overenthusiastic after the success of April or were displaying naivety, panic or sheer greed by trying to stage too many races too quickly. Even for the hunting fraternity, with a long tradition of holding steeplechases, such events were usually annual affairs. Ironically, the hot weather that summer could also have been a factor in keeping spectators away. Perhaps the cool sea-breezes would have been a far more attractive proposition than a dusty trek from Caebricks up to the racecourse. This view seems to be confirmed by a letter written to *The Cambrian* two years after the demise of the racecourse, noting how the Mumbles had profited when attractions such as Manselton had been advertised:

That event was advertised by the railway companies, having a special line on their posters in reference to the 'Swansea Races'. A large number who availed themselves of the cheap trains did *not* go to the races, but made much of the opportunity to visit the Mumbles.[6]

Like many other racecourses in Britain, Manselton may have introduced too many hybrid programmes, where steeplechases, flat and hurdle races all took place together. The only place where such a programme really worked was Aintree which possessed the finest steeplechase course in the world and where the Grand National was always able to excite extraordinary interest. Manselton could not hope to compete with such an event.

Whatever the reason for the lack of support, the August 1887 meeting seems to have been a turning point in the fortunes of the Manselton course. The third meeting of the year took place on Boxing Day, supplemented by pony, galloway and trotting races later in the week. The prize money of £455 for six races was substantially down on August, yet even so was above average for provincial steeplechase meetings at this time.

The Executive was floundering in a vicious circle. They had not been able to raise enough money from gate receipts in August to put up as much prize money as they would have wished for the Christmas meeting and poor attendance on Boxing Day meant a loss that would jeopardise any future funding. Even the local gentry, despite a 'goodly gathering' on the course, could no longer be counted on and *The Cambrian* regretfully announced the postponement of the Swansea Race Ball. Its report also confirmed the fate of the racecourse –

SWANSEA TOWN LIBERAL ASSOCIATION.
POLICY OF THE PRESENT GOVERNMENT.

MR. LABOUCHERE, M.P..
WILL ADDRESS A PUBLIC MEETING
IN THE ALBERT HALL,
ON THURSDAY, the 5th of JANUARY, 1888, at 8 p.m.

TICKETS OF ADMISSION :—Reserved Seats, Area (numbered) and Balcony (unnumbered), 2s.; Unreserved
Area, Balcony, and Orchestra, 1s.; Promenade, 6d.; Gallery, 3d.; may be had from A. W. HALDEN, Secretary,
Liberal Club; and following District Secretaries—MR. THOMAS GUTHERIDGE, St. Helen's Avenue; MR. J.
CONIBEAR, 37, Oxford-street; MR. LEWIS HARRIS, 126, High-street; MR. JOSEPH THOMAS, 41, Henrietta-
street; MR. EVAN J. THOMAS, 8, Portia-terrace; MR. G. W. DAVIE, 203, Kensington-terrace; MR. FRED J.
DAVIES, Pentregethin, Cwmbwrla; MR. GEO. WILLIAMS, 13, Kilvey-terrace. Early application necessary.[3372

SWANSEA RACE BALL.

THIS BALL,

ANNOUNCED TO TAKE PLACE ON

DECEMBER 26TH, 1887.

HAS BEEN

POSTPONED UNTIL EASTER.   [3234

SWANSEA HOSPITAL BALL.

THE TWENTIETH ANNUAL BALL,
In aid of the Funds of the Swansea Hospital,

The Christmas week edition of *The Cambrian, 1887.* Despite announcing the postponement
of the Swansea Race Ball, the paper is still advertising Christmas Trotting Races, and a
Grand Foot Race, on December 29th, and the Great Western Railway are offering cheap
third-class return tickets for the Boxing Day races.

(Courtesy Swansea Reference Library)

The Swansea Christmas racing week was brought to a conclusion yesterday, the trotting races resulting in another fiasco. We write this in sorrow, and almost shame – that an enterprise which has been undertaken and carried out with so much spirit should apparently be boycotted by the inhabitants of Swansea and South Wales is almost beyond belief.[7]

The key to the debacle appears to lie in the hands of just one man, the mysterious Arthur Burr. He was one of the purchasers of the life interest in the income from land of Sir Richard Mansel Mansel and had quite probably sweet-talked the baronet into ploughing £1,200 of rents and profits into the racecourse scheme rather than on the upkeep of his estates. It was he who probably persuaded Sir Richard to mortgage the future rents of lands that he owned, thereby raising additional funds of £24,000 to finance the venture.

Little wonder, then, that when Burr appeared before the Bankruptcy Court in Lincoln's Inn in November 1891, there was an altercation between him and Mr Beyfus, the barrister appearing for the Trustees of the Mansel Estates. The latter would have regarded Burr as a contemptible con man who had exploited Mansel's weaknesses and played a major part in his ruination. Since the petition for liquidation in 1883, Burr had managed Mansel's affairs, allowing him £1,500 a year until he had cleared the estates. During the late 1880s that amount had fluctuated but he had no legal claim against Burr for the allowance because it had only been a verbal arrangement. The baronet was putty in the trickster's greasy paws.[8] The examination of Burr's affairs revealed that the Swansea Racecourse scheme had made a loss of £50,000. Burr estimated that he had paid £30,000 of this but was still liable for another £20,000. Quite who the creditors were will never be known, because Arthur Burr absconded, along with the records of accounts from the Manselton Estate Office. Mansel House in Courtenay Street, indeed, had been the local base for his Landed Estates Agency, which he had established in the early 1880s, seemingly with the help of two gentlemen called Frank Manley Cobbett and Harvey Weller Richards. The trio appeared many times in an unending stream of cases involving the Agency and the Trustees of the various Mansel estates. By 1885 he had disposed of the business for £60,000, which surely should have covered his losses! The demise of the company coincided with the date of the failure of the racecourse in 1887. What is scarcely believable is Burr's claim that he took the liabilities of the Agency on his own shoulders, 'as he did not wish his friends to suffer' and had paid the £30,000 in calls on shares. For, having sold it two years previously, he would have had no legal liability. This would seem to indicate that the 'sale' was not as straightforward as it appeared, perhaps a legal smokescreen to keep creditors and trustees at bay. Burr's gross liabilities were put at £344,989, although only £49,066 were expected to claim after the waiving of two creditors' debts. He estimated his assets at £77,903 after the payment of preferential debts, thus giving him a surplus of £28,837. He maintained that his property ought to realise at least sufficient to pay 20s. in the pound. At the close of evidence Mr Registrar Giffard allowed the debtor to pass his examination.[9]

Burr had been summonsed in March 1891 at Swansea Police Court, together with his business partner Frederick Lovell Keays, by the Overseers of Penderry for the non-payment of rates on the Manselton course. Several attempts to collect the arrears from the two, who were jointly assessed, had failed and the case could not be proceeded with against Burr because he had moved address and therefore could not be served with the summons. Keays, too, was absent through illness but Mr Emmott from London, speaking on his behalf, claimed that his client had never been the owner of the racecourse but had merely lent Mr Burr money which he had never got back. He contended that Mr Burr was the owner, having admitted as much in a speech quoted in the *Southern Free Press and East Greenwich Times*. At the adjourned hearing a fortnight later Keays made an appearance, again denying his liability and stating that he had no interest in the course. Burr promptly 'sold him out' by sending a letter to the court, claiming that all leases had been made in Keays's name. No honour amongst thieves it would seem! The magistrates had visibly lost patience with Burr when he sent another letter to the hearing on 13th May, accusing him of throwing every obstacle in the way during the previous two years. Despite having to pay the costs of the day, and with arrears of £100 hanging over him, the hearing was once more adjourned. An appeal was then lodged against the rating of £200 a year on the grounds that the racecourse had been discontinued. This was accepted and a new valuation of £58 for agricultural purposes agreed upon. Whether he troubled the court again is not known! By June, Keays had been declared bankrupt and the public examination of the affairs of Frank Manley Cobbett fixed for the 21st October. Of his total debts of £12,000 he put £500 down to his involvement with the Swansea Racecourse.[10]

If Burr and Keays were a pair of bad apples, it certainly seems that the Executive Committee – and for that matter, Sir Richard Mansel – were innocent, if gullible, pawns in their game. By the end of 1887 the Manselton Executive had all but collapsed and Arthur Burr had disappeared into the dust cloud.

After the Christmas meeting of 1887 there was no more racing at Manselton until the Autumn Steeplechases of 1888. In early September a local committee, including some who had officiated at Clyne, met at the Cameron Arms with a view to arranging a steeplechase meeting the following month. Over £120 had already been subscribed, the half guinea entitling members to a ticket to the ground and paddock as well as exclusive access to the private stand and enclosure. It was decided that if the meeting proved to be a financial success, a fund would be formed at one of the local banks as a nucleus for future meetings. The ever-supportive *Cambrian* urged people to attend:

> The abandonment of the excellent course at Manselton would be a matter of regret, and to prevent any such contingency the horse-loving community of Swansea should do its utmost to

Swansea and South Wales Steeplechases

The last significant advertisement for a major horse racing fixture – *The Cambrian*, October 1888
(Courtesy Swansea Reference Library)

swell the subscriptions list, should put in an appearance at Manselton on 18th October, and do all they can to promote the success of the meeting.[11]

Despite good sport and brilliant weather, attendance at the meeting was poor, and the explanation given by *The Cambrian* – that 'the site . . . was too far away, and considered by many to be at the wrong end of town' – would have convinced no-one.[12] Despite huge crowds initially, the unpalatable truth was that the Races could not attract a sufficiently large number of paying spectators. The consumers had made their choice and the venture had collapsed.

Those October races seem to have been the last steeplechases held at Manselton. One last effort was made in June 1889 but these were organised by the Clyne Committee and were advertised as the Clyne Valley Races for ponies and galloways. Attendance was poor, the grandstand presenting 'a beggarly array of empty seats.'[11] Officially, horse racing on the Manselton course had come to an end after barely two years. The ill-fated ground was used for other events, however. The Manselton Fete was held there in May 1888, attracting a crowd of thousands to watch a variety of famous acts.

MANSELTON FETE – IT WENT OFF WITH GREAT *ÉCLAT!*

. . . The entertainment included the Klos and Espaliers trapeze artists, Madame Carlini and her troupe of performing dogs and monkeys, as well as the spectacular launch of an air balloon which a Mr Simons piloted safely into Somerset. No sooner had the intrepid aeronaut vanished into hot air than the 'African Blondin' appeared on a rope sixty feet above the astonished crowd. Here, he proceeded to light a stove, cook his dinner, drive a wheelbarrow along and as a grand finale, cross from one end to the other blindfolded. In the evening the crowd was treated to a grand display of fireworks – and the band of Third Glamorgan Rifle Volunteers.

(The Cambrian, May 25th, 1888)

DESTRUCTION OF THE GRANDSTAND

One creditor who'd had enough of Burr and his friends was Richard Richards. By a written agreement of 30th November 1886 he had granted a lease of a portion of the racecourse at a yearly rent of £39 7s 6d to Burr and Keays, land which the promoters needed to build their grandstand. In March 1887 sale of this land had been agreed in writing, but the purchase had never been completed. When the case came to court in March 1891, it transpired that no rent had been paid since September 1889. As plaintiff, Richard Richards was seeking an injunction to restrain the defendants (who included Burr, Keays, Cobbett, Mansel and Burnard) from removing the grandstand and iron gate-railings fixed to the freehold, arguing that they were trespassing on his land. Shortly before the action was brought, the defendants had taken up the old fences and hedges on Richards's portion of land and erected a large iron and wood fence. According to David Jenkins, one of the firm of builders who had constructed it, they had 'practically removed' the grandstand, causing £500 worth of damage. They had also begun to take up the iron railings. The defence arguement was that the grandstand and fence were not permanent structures affixed to the freehold, but were trade fixtures brought upon the premises for the purpose of carrying on the business of a racecourse and could be removed accordingly. However, the judge directed the jury that the grandstand *was* a fixture in the freehold. Until the next sittings of the Glamorganshire Assizes the defendants were not to remove any more of the grandstand or railings, at which time a decision would be made about damages payable to Richards.

(The Cambrian, March 20th and 27th, 1891)

Foot racing, coursing and whippet racing continued to be held at the course, the latter until well into the twentieth century. By that time the grandstand, the oak gates, posts and all of the other features that had been so beautifully crafted by a highly skilled local workforce had long gone – presumably sold in the 1890s to raise capital and pay off some of the creditors. Undoubtedly many an 'unofficial' horse race took place on the old course until the building of houses in Penlan after the Second World War. The hill above Manselton is still known as 'The Racecourse' but many locals would be surprised to learn that it was such a big undertaking.

Whatever Arthur Burr was about – and the motives of this mysterious, shady man will never be fully known or understood – there is no doubt that in 1887 he succeeded in bringing to Swansea the most spectacular horse racing the town had ever seen. Such glory has never come again.

Present day: the southern edge of Penlan overlooking Manselton where only the railings remain, to remind us of the once splendid racecourse

(Courtesy the author)

References

CHAPTER 1

1 Glanmor Williams (ed.), *Swansea, An Illustrated History* (1990), p.73
2 John Davies and G. E. Mingay, 'Agriculture in an Industrial Environment', in *Glamorgan County History, Vol V, Industrial Glamorgan 1700 – 1970*, ed. Arthur H. John and Glanmor Williams (1980), p.292 – 293
3 *The Cambrian*, 1-4-1887
4 Wray Vamplew, *Pay Up and Play the Game: Professional Sport in Britain, 1875 –1914* (1988), p.52
5 Gareth Williams, 'Sport and Society in Glamorgan, 1750 – 1980', in *Glamorgan County History, Vol VI, Glamorgan Society 1780 – 1980* (1988), p.385
6 W. R. Lambert, *Drink and Society in Victorian Wales, c1820 – 1920* (1983), p.12
7 F. M. L. Thompson, *The Rise of Respectable Society*, (1988), p.276 – 277

CHAPTER 2

1 David Boorman, *The Brighton of Wales: Swansea as a Fashionable Resort, c1780 – c1830* (1986), p.2
2 *The Cambrian*, 16-4-1808
3 *The Cambrian*, (advertisement) 5-4-1806 and 23-4-1808
4 E. I. Spence, *Summer Excursions through Parts of Oxfordshire, Gloucestershire, Warwickshire, Staffordshire, Herefordshire, Derbyshire and South Wales* (1809), p.127
5 *The Cambrian*, 21-7-1810
6 ibid. 21-7-1810
7 ibid. 10-5-1823
8 ibid. 21-6-1834 and 12-7-1834
9 ibid. 21-6-1834 and 12-7-1834 (advertisement)
10 ibid. 19-6-1841
11 ibid. 20-8-1847
12 Glanmor Williams (ed.), *Swansea, an Illustrated History* (1990), p.89
13 A Native, *Reminiscences of Old Swansea* (1902,) p.10 – 11
14 Earl of Suffolk, *Racing and Steeplechasing* (1886), p.246
15 *The Swansea Journal*, 13-9-1856
16 *The Cambrian*, 24-8-1855

CHAPTER 3

1 *The Cambrian*, 27-7-1860
2 ibid. 24-5-1861
3 ibid. 31-8-1866
4 ibid. 21-10-1870
5 ibid. 21-10-1870
6 ibid. 8-10-1886
7 ibid. 25-5-1888
8 ibid. 11-5-1894, 18-5-1894, 10-8-1894
9 ibid. 21-12-1894 (supplement), 26-4-1895, 30-8-1895
10 *The South Wales Daily Post*, 17-5-1910
11 ibid. 1-8-1924 and 5-8-1924
12 ibid. 3-8-1927
13 Leonard Jayne, *Pony Racing: including the story of Northolt Park*, undated.

CHAPTER 4

1 Roger Munting, *Hedges and Hurdles: A Social and Economic History of National Hunt Racing* (1987), p.2-3
2 Michael Seth Smith, Peter Willett, Roger Mortimer and John Lawrence, *The History of Steeplechasing* (1966), p.16
3 R Longrigg, *The History of Horse Racing* (1972) – quoting *New Sporting Magazine* (April 1840)
4 *The Liverpool Mercury*, 1-3-1839
5 Roger Munting, op. cit. p.21
6 R. S. Surtees, *Plain or Ringlets* (1860), p.533

CHAPTER 5

1 *The Cambrian*, 24-12-1886
2 ibid. 18-3-1887
3 ibid. 1-4-1887
4 ibid. 22-7-1887
5 ibid. 8-4-1887 (advertisement)
6 ibid. 29-4-1887
7 ibid. 1-4-1887

[8] ibid. 5-8-1887

[9] Wray Vamplew, *The Turf: A Social and Economic History of Horse Racing* (1976), p.40 – 41

[10] *The Cambrian*, 15-4-1887

[11] ibid. 5-8-1887, 30-12-1887, plus *Racing Calendar, 1887: Steeple Chase* p.425 – 426

[12] ibid. 19-10-1888

[13] ibid. 5-8-1887

[14] ibid. 15-4-1887

[15] ibid. 22-4-1887

[16] ibid. 5-8-1887

[17] ibid. 30-12-1887

[18] ibid. 5-8-1887

[19] ibid. 5-8-1887

[20] Information from Miss James, Manselton Estate Office

[21] Advertisement in *The Cambrian* 29-7-1887

CHAPTER 6

[1] Wray Vamplew, *A Social and Economic History of Horse Racing*, (1976) p45

[2] Alun Richards, *A Touch of Glory* (1980), p.40; David Farmer, *The All Whites* (1995), p.4 and p.12; David Farmer, *Swansea City 1912 – 1982* (1982), p.16

[3] Quoted in Wray Vamplew, p.44

[4] *The Cambrian*, 22-7-1887

[5] ibid. 5-8-1887

[6] ibid. 27-3-1891

[7] ibid. 30-12-1887

[8] ibid. 31-7-1891

[9] *The Times*, 13-11-1891 and 11-11-1891, also *The Cambrian*, 20-11-1891

[10] *The Cambrian*, 20-3-1891, 3-4-1891, 15-5-1891, 5-6-1891, 12-6-1891, 23-10-1891

[11] ibid. 14-9-1888

[12] ibid. 19-10-1888

[13] ibid. 14-6-1889

Select Bibliography

PRIMARY SOURCES

The Cambrian, 1803 – 1899,
The Hall Day Minute Book, 20- 9-1822
The Swansea Journal, 1843, 1844, 1856, 1857
The Liverpool Mercury, 1839
The Times, 1883, 1891
The South Wales Daily Post, 1910, 1914, 1924, 1927

BOOKS AND SECONDARY SOURCES_

Best, Geoffrey, *Mid-Victorian Britain, 1851-75*, Fontana Press, 1977.
Boorman, David, *The Brighton of Wales, Swansea as a Fashionable Resort c. 1780-1830*, Swansea, 1986.
Chesney, Kellow *The Victorian Underworld*, Readers Union Ltd, Newton Abbot, 1970.
Farmer, David, *The All Whites, the Life and Times of Swansea RFC*, DFPS, Swansea, 1995.
Gabb, Gerald, *Jubilee Swansea II, the town and its people in the 1890s*, Gerald Gabb, 1999.
Harrison, Brian, *Drink and the Victorians*, Faber and Faber, 1971.
Howell, David W, *Patriarchs and Parasites (The Gentry of South-West Wales in the Eighteenth Century)*, Cardiff University Press, 1986.
Hunt, EH, *Regional Wage Variations in Britain 1850–1914*, Clarendon Press, Oxford, 1973.
Jayne, Leonard, *Pony Racing: including the story of Northolt Park*, Hutchinson, undated.
Jones, Tecwyn Vaughan, 'Bando' in *Llafar Gwlad* Rhif 8, 30 Mehefin, 1985.
Lambert, WR, *Drink and Sobriety in Victorian Wales c. 1820-1895*, University of Wales Press, 1983.
Longrigg, Roger,*The History of Horse Racing*, Macmillan, 1972.
Morgan, Prys (editor), *Glamorgan County History, Volume VI, Glamorgan Society 1780-1980*, Glamorgan County History Trust Ltd, 1988.
Mortimer, Roger, *The Jockey Club*, Cassell, 1958.
Munting, Roger, *Hedges and Hurdles, A Social and Economic History of National Hunt Racing*, JA Allen, London, 1987.
Native A , 'Reminiscences of Old Swansea', reprinted from *The Cambrian*, 1902.
Richards, Alun, *A Touch of Glory* , Michael Joseph, 1980.
Rogers, WC, *A Pictorial History of Swansea*, Gomer Press, 1981.

Smith, Michael Seth; Willett, Peter; Mortimer, Roger; Lawrence, John, *The History of Steeplechasing*, Michael Joseph, 1966.

Spence, EI, *Summer Excursions Through Parts of Oxfordshire, Gloucestershire, Warwickshire, Staffordshire, Herefordshire, Derbyshire and South Wales*, London (2nd Edition), 1809.

Suffolk, Earl of, *Racing and Steeplechasing*,The Badminton Library, Longmans, 1886.

Surtees, RS, *Plain or Ringlets*, The Folio Society, 1986, (originally 1860).

Thompson, FML, *The Rise of Respectable Society*, Fontana, London, 1988.

Vamplew, Wray, *Pay Up and Play the Game: Professional Sport in Britain 1875-1914*, Cambridge University Press, 1988.

Vamplew, Wray, *The Turf: A Social and Economic History of Horse Racing*, Allen Lane, 1976.

Weatherby, Messrs, *The Racing Calendar*, 1774 onwards.

Weatherby, Messrs, *The Racing Calendar (Steeple Chases)*, 1886 onwards.

Williams, Glanmor (editor), *Swansea, An Illustrated History*, Christopher Davies, Swansea, 1990.

Williams, Glanmor and John, Arthur H, *Glamorgan County History, Volume V, Industrial Glamorgan 1700-1870*, Glamorgan County History Trust Ltd, 1980.

Williams, Y Parch,W. Samlet, *Hanes a Hynafiaethau Llansamlet*, E.W. Evans, Dolgellau, 1908.

OFFICIAL DOCUMENTS

Her Majesty's Stationery Office, *Census of England and Wales 1901 (63 VICT. C.4)*, Love and Malcolmson, 1902.